Robert O'Neill

INTERACTION

Practice modules at the First Certificate level

Longman

Longman Group Limited
London

*Associated companies, branches and
representatives throughout the world*

© Longman Group Ltd. 1976

All rights reserved. No part of this publication may be reproduced, stored in a retrieval system, or transmitted in any form or by any means, electronic, mechanical, photocopying, recording, or otherwise, without the prior permission of the Copyright owner.

First published 1976
New impression 1978

ISBN 0 582 55243 5

Filmset by Keyspools Limited, Golborne, Lancashire

Printed in Hong Kong by
The Hong Kong Printing Press (1977) Ltd

Contents

	page
To the Teacher	vii
Section One: Stories and Dialogues	1
1·1 Smash-Up	3
1·2 'Hard Times'	7
1·3 A Dangerous Place	11
1·4 A Quarrel	15
1·5 The Opinion Survey	19
1·6 A Wonderful Chance	23
1·7 A Bad Way to Begin a Marriage	27
1·8 Rivals	31
1·9 Unlucky with Women	35
1·10 Two Strangers on a Train	39
Section Two: Interviews	43
2·1 The Powerful and the Famous	45
2·2 To Smoke or Not to Smoke?	49
2·3 The King of Bad Taste	53
2·4 Football Hooliganism	57
2·5 White Death	61
Section Three: Listening Comprehension	65
3·1 Escape from Hanley Park	67
3·2 A Double Life	69
3·3 Prince Albert and the Jewel Robbers	71
3·4 The Prize (1)	73
3·5 The Prize (2)	75
3·6 The Prize (3)	77
3·7 A Slight Emergency	79
3·8 The Room	81
3·9 Interprop Limited	83
3·10 Arrival	85
Supplement: Listening Comprehension Passages	

For Maya van Horn

List of Functions

Describing an accident, 4
Reporting questions, 4
Threats and promises, 6
Describing a town or city, 8
Certain and uncertain plans, 8
Two ways of getting information, 10
Awkward questions, 10
Describing people, 12
Warnings, 12
Repeating questions, pressing for more information, 14
Reporting warnings, 14
Apologising, 16
Describing difficulties, 16
Accusations, 18
Denials, 18
Suggestions, 18
Describing a job, 20
Instructions, 20
Questions you don't really understand, 22
More ways of asking 'delicate' questions and making requests, 22
Reporting refusals, 22
Describing a course of study, etc., 24
Orders and advice, 26
Reporting orders and advice, 26
Rejecting advice, 26
Describing the weather, 28
Excuses, 28
'Giving in' unwillingly, 30
Obligations, duties, responsibilities, 30
Future arrangements, 30
Expressing suspicion, 34
Reporting what they said, 34
Congratulations, 34
Describing likes and dislikes, 36
Invitations, 36
Turning down invitations, 38
Accepting invitations and getting the time and place right, 38
Describing food, 40
Expressing doubt, 42

Showing you are almost certain, 42
Asking for permission, 42
Describing people's reactions, 47
Insisting on things, 48
Reporting it, 48
Contrasts and comparisons, 51
Describing habits, 51
Disagreeing, 52
Agreeing, 52
Not being 100 per cent certain about what you remember, 55
Describing an audience's reactions, 55
Disapproval, 56
Approving/not disapproving, 56
Opinions/proposals, 59
Describing how you feel about the way other people behave, 59
Getting people's opinions, 60
Reporting proposals, 60
Saying things you think people may not believe, 63
Correcting people, 63
Describing fear, terror, etc., 63
Expressing opinions you suspect may be wrong, 64
Expressing suppositions rather than definite facts, 68
Surprise and astonishment, 70
Showing anger at the way other people treat you, 72
Complaining – showing that you don't understand the point of things, 74
Expressing gratitude and appreciation (formal), 78
Telling people to do things in a calm, reassuring way, 80
Showing that you are disappointed, that you expected something different, 82
Getting people to be more precise, 84
Suggesting that someone has made a mistake, 86

Acknowledgements

Like most other people involved in English as a Foreign Language, I must acknowledge the contribution of David Wilkins towards clarifying what is essentially a shift of emphasis: instead of a rigidly-defined grammatical progression this book rests upon a scheme first of notional and communicative categories and then a selection of the structures needed to express them. But I have not interpreted Wilkins and others to mean that grammatical progressions should be entirely abandoned! The structures needed to express these notions are *also* selected on partly intuitive criteria as to learnability and an ascending order of structural complexity.

I am particularly grateful to my friends and ex-colleagues, Rene Richterich, Ottomar Willecke, Gilbert Dalgaglian and Margaret Niethammer-Stott, with whom I worked in Zurich. At that time, more than seven years ago, they were insisting on and defining the need for a more communicative order of grammatical structure.

I must also mention the work of Dr. R. D. Laing, the psychologist and social philosopher. Anyone who is seriously interested in how language is really used in communication must study and be aware of the ambiguities in it which he and others expound.

Last of all, I must acknowledge the great help that Jake Allsop gave in discussing and testing the manuscript as well as the many useful suggestions he gave.

Robert O'Neill
Hove, England
Hanover, Germany
Hollywood, USA
1974–76

To the Teacher

Main aims of the book

Who is this book for?
Interaction has two main aims:
1 to give training and practice in a wide range of communicative language skills that are necessary for any student who wants to use English efficiently;
2 to achieve the first aim in such a way that the learner is also prepared for the Cambridge First Certificate or other similar examinations for students of English as a foreign language.

Minimum previous knowledge

Before the book can be used successfully, learners should have had *at least* 3 years of weekly double-lessons at an adult education centre, or be in their fifth year of English study at a secondary school, or have reached *an equivalent stage*. In other words they should be at a level corresponding to the end of *Kernel Lessons Intermediate* or *Practice and Progress* or its alternative *Mainline Progress A and B*.

Entry knowledge in terms of grammatical structure

The following is a list of forms which learners should be able to *use*, if not always perfectly, before they begin to use this material:

simple and progressive forms of present and past (He *comes* here every day. He *is coming* now. He *came* here yesterday. He *was coming* here when she saw him.)

present perfect, present perfect progressive, past perfect (I'*ve been* ill. I'*ve been feeling* ill. I'*d been* to the doctor's before you came.)

main future forms (I'*ll be* 25 next week. I'*m giving* a party. It's *going to be* a good party.)

passive in future, present, perfect and past (It *will be done*. It *is done* all the time. It *has* already *been done*. It *was done*.)

type 1 and 2 conditionals (*Will* you *go* if I *do*? *Would* you *go* if I *did*?)

basic adjective and adverb constructions (She's a *good* swimmer. She swims *well*. I'm a *fairly good* swimmer. You swim *very badly*.)

basic gerund constructions (I *enjoy swimming*. I'm not *used to swimming* in such cold water. *Swimming is* a good sport.)

connectors and subordinators (I'm sure *that* I'll drown. *Unless* you help me, I'll drown. He drowned *because* he was a bad swimmer. *When* he went under, I tried to save him, etc.)

the main modal verbs (*can, could, will, would, should, shall, ought to, must, have (got) to, had better, needn't, may, might*.)

comparative and superlative constructions (He *speaks as well as* you do. His English *is as good as* yours. He *speaks better/more fluently* than you do. His English *is better/more fluent than* yours. He was *the most intelligent* student I ever had.)

This, in rough terms, is the *minimum entry* knowledge before *Interaction* can be used effectively. And it is assumed that although learners must have a basic fluency with these forms – that is, be able to recognise and use the forms without too much struggle – they will use them only with a *very limited communicative range*.

Efficient communication

An example of this is that learners may know how to ask 'straight questions' (*How much do you earn?*) but not how to phrase such questions so that they cause minimum offence (*Do you mind if I ask how much you earn? Excuse me, but would you mind if I asked?*) Or when they want to suggest that other people should not do things, they tend to sound as if they were giving orders (*Don't do that. You should do that!*) rather than polite advice (*If I were you, I don't think I would do that.*). And when they disagree they tend to use blunt forms like *You're wrong* rather than *Are you sure that's right?* or *Aren't you perhaps making a mistake?*

Using the appropriate form is not a matter of social etiquette, but of efficient communication. *Interaction* sets out to help learners toward efficient communication in English, in both spoken and written forms. Efficient communication can be defined as making sure not only that the basic contents of what you say are understood but also that you do not at the same time give a false impression of their implications and of your relationship to the person you are talking to. Efficient communication in this sense is also a basic skill required by the First Certificate examination.

Structure of the book

What kind of material is in *Interaction*?
Interaction has three main Sections:
Section 1: Stories and Dialogues (ten Units each of four pages)
Section 2: Interviews (five Units each of four pages)
Section 3: Listening Comprehension (ten Units each of two pages)

Special note about Section 3

The passages for listening comprehension themselves are *not* in Section 3, but in a booklet inserted into the back of the book. The passages can be taken out and given to the class after the Unit has been done. The ten Units in this Section contain comprehension and exercise material based on each passage.

Recorded materials

Certain parts of each Unit in each Section have been recorded and are marked with the symbol ⊕.

These parts are:
in Section 1: the dialogue of each Unit (always on the third page of the Unit)
in Section 2: the interviews themselves (always the first two pages)
in Section 3: the passages (in the booklet inserted into the back of the book)

The use of these recordings (on reel-to-reel tape or cassette) is completely *optional*. *Interaction* can be used without them. However, the variety of voices and accents, the real-life quality of the dialogues and interviews and the dramatic but simple presentation of the passages for Section 3 are of great help in maintaining interest and furthering listening comprehension in general.

More information about each Section is always given in the two-page introduction for the student before each Section.

Modules of material rather than a 'book'

How can Interaction be used?
Interaction has been designed as a *system of modules* of material and not as a book to be worked through from beginning to end. Instead, modules of material should be composed. A typical module of material would consist of:

  2 Units from Section 1
  1 Unit from Section 2
  2 Units from Section 3
  ─────────
  = 5 Units of material (for the one module)

How to compose a module

Such a module should be worked through before the next module is begun. It is extremely simple to compose these modules. The following diagram shows a suggested composition for all five modules. The Unit numbers always begin with the number of the Section. Thus, Unit 2.3 is Section 2, Unit 3.

	Module 1	Module 2	Module 3	Module 4	Module 5
	1.1, 1.2	1.3, 1.4	1.5, 1.6	1.7, 1.8	1.9, 1.10
	2.1	2.2	2.3	2.4	2.5
	3.1, 3.2	3.3, 3.4	3.5, 3.6	3.7, 3.8	3.9, 3.10

Time

You will probably need at least 10 teaching hours ('contact hours') for each module, or between 50–60 contact hours for all 5 modules. The modules can of course be extended; teachers may add either their own materials or those taken from other sources.

Other books that can be used with *Interaction*

In other words, *Interaction* is designed as the *core* of a modular learning system. For the sake of convenience, *Interaction* is presented in book form but is not designed to be used rigidly as a book. Other books may be used with *Interaction*. For example, *Insight* (Donn Byrne and Susan Holden, Longman 1976) and *Interaction* are designed to complement each other, though each can stand on its own. If there is a need for remedial intensive structure practice, books like W. S. Allen's *Living English Structure*, Pit Corder's *Intermediate Practice Book* or Gordon Drummond's *English Structure Practice* and for remedial composition practice, D. H. Spencer's small but very good *Guided Composition Exercises*, as well as the *Longman Integrated Comprehension and Composition* series (Stages 5 and 6) will be found handy and effective aids. (All the above are Longman titles.) Penguin's *Connections* series is an excellent source of additional composition and discussion. Teachers may find *A Communicative Grammar of English* by Geoffrey Leech and Jan Svartvik (Longman) extremely useful for their own reference.

Tests

For teachers who want 'mock-exam' passages as part of the general preparation for students for the examination, two separate test packs are available, *Practice Tests 'A' and 'B' for FCE candidates* (Longman). These were originally produced to accompany *Mainline Skills A and B* but have now been packaged separately and can be used at the end of *Interaction*.

Flexibility and variety principles of design

Interaction is designed as a simple but sophisticated and flexible system for use in different parts of the world and for a variety of teaching situations. It is based on three specific design principles.
1 The different skills required for the First Certificate and for communication in general require a variety of teaching and learning strategies and approaches.
2 Student-centred learning means, among other things, that groups of learners must be able to interact with each other as much as possible and not only with the teacher.
3 Teaching is not the same as testing.

Interaction sets out to fulfil these principles by providing:
1 a variety of different materials to develop the different skills;
2 a great deal of opportunity for learners to interview, discuss and take different roles with each other;
3 material that does *not* imitate the style or form of the First Certificate papers but *does* develop the skills required by those papers through teaching and not testing strategies.

Specific suggestions about methodology

More specific *suggestions* to the teacher and *advice* to the learner are provided in the two page introduction to each Section.

Section One *Stories and Dialogues*

Some of the people in this section

1
George, who has a bad experience in a car

2
George, who has to see his boss about something important

3
Paula, a journalist in a dangerous place

4
Mike, a young man in a terrible hurry

5
Carol, who does what some people think is a very strange job

6
Janet, who is afraid to tell her father something

7
John and Anna, who have a problem on their honeymoon

8
Alison and Marcia in a big race

9
Denis, who always has terrible luck with women

10
Kate, a girl just back from South America, who meets a stranger on a train

What this section contains	This section has ten Units of material. Each Unit consists of one story (first page); one page of comprehension, vocabulary, interaction and language practice (second page); one dialogue which continues or expands the story + exercises (third page); one page of further practice and composition and dialogue writing (fourth page).
This section deals with the skills of	Reading comprehension (Paper 2); Use of English (Paper 3, Section B); Composition (Paper 1).
Some of the things you will learn in this section	Among other things in this section, you will learn ways of making promises (and also threats) asking questions you think the other person may not want to answer showing that you have not understood things or need still more information giving advice, and also orders making suggestions and requests

talking about future plans
expressing doubt
making accusations and denying them
showing you will do something but don't really want to.

Suggestions to the teacher

It is for you to decide which techniques and general approach are most suited for your particular learning-group. The following notes simply suggest possible presentation and practice strategies.

The picture that begins each Unit
This is simply a visual lead-in, designed to arouse interest in and focus attention on the story before it is read, as well as stimulate discussion. Let the class look at it for some time. Do not be afraid of silence at first. Encourage speculation about what is happening in the picture and why. There is no particular 'correct' answer for this first set of questions.

The questions about the story itself
These are particularly important as a means of focusing attention on *general comprehension goals*, which is why they must be studied before the text is read. Always return to them immediately after this. At this stage, discourage questions about the meaning of particular words, and see whether or not the *general details* of the story have been understood even if a few words have not. It is essential that students learn such 'general comprehension' techniques for the examination itself.

Presenting the story itself
This has not been recorded. It can sometimes be read silently by the class, and perhaps at other times read aloud by you as the class listens with books closed.

Presenting the dialogue
This has been recorded and lends itself in particular to aural presentation. The class may benefit at times if they quickly read the dialogue text first, although this is not always necessary. The open-ended dialogues that accompany the dialogue itself (right-hand of same page) are particularly useful in encouraging speculative and 'free' language work.

Doing the exercises and homework
Homework possibilities, as noted before, are *Related Practice* (right-hand side, *second* page) and the bottom right-hand side of the *fourth* page. The other exercises are recommended mainly for *oral work in class*. Note in particular the exercises under the heading *Interaction*. These exercises always give scope for role-playing and other forms of interaction between students in either group or paired work. Always make sure that answers are given to the questions the students have to ask, for example page 12.

Special language notes on the dialogues

1.1c
'bloody', although no longer absolutely taboo is still regarded as insulting and 'rough' language.

1.3c
both policemen speak colloquial American. In standard British English 'I got a theft' would be '*I've got* a theft' and 'I *gotta* write all this down' would be 'I've got to write all this down'.

1·1a SMASH-UP

Look at the picture and discuss

Describe what you can see in the picture.

Why do you think the man is so angry?

Suppose you had caused an accident like this. What would you do? Give reasons.
a) Stop and try to help.
b) Drive away as quickly as possible.

Pre-questions for the text

Two men, Howard and George are mentioned in the story. What do you learn about them?

Whose fault do you think the accident shown in the picture was? Give reasons.

'The last time I lent you my car, you smashed it up,' Howard said. 'But that was years ago, and it wasn't even my fault!' George answered angrily. They were brothers. Howard had never trusted George very much. And he was especially proud of his new car.

'Why did you say you wanted to borrow it?' Howard asked again. 'I have to take Linda to see her grandmother this Saturday. My own car is being repaired and it won't be ready in time,' George explained, trying to keep his temper. Linda was George's fiancée. Her grandmother lived out in the country.

'Oh, come on. It's the least one brother can do for another,' George said. He knew Howard did not need the car himself that weekend. Howard was obviously very unhappy with the idea. 'Oh, all right. But for God's sake be careful!' he finally said after a long pause.

It was cold but sunny that Saturday. There were icy patches on the road.

'My grandmother's place shouldn't be too far now,' Linda said. They were on a narrow country road and George was driving very carefully. Howard had told him not to take any risks. The car in front of them was going very slowly, and was keeping to the centre of the road. George could see the driver, a middle-aged and very thin man. He was pointing out things to an old woman next to him. George tried to relax and keep cool. It was dangerous to overtake, so he slowed down and kept a safe distance between himself and the car in front.

The car in front disappeared around a sharp bend. When George came round it, he saw that it had stopped in the middle of the road. The driver was pointing to an old farmhouse. George swerved, skidded off the road, and crashed into an iron fence. He and Linda were badly shaken-up and stunned, but she was unhurt. His forehead was bleeding. The damage to the car, however, was terrible. The front lights had been smashed, the bonnet was dented and one mudguard had been torn away. George stumbled out onto the road, cursing. But the other car, a large green Jaguar, was driving away in the distance.

1·1b

Text: comprehension and discussion

Multiple choice comprehension
Choose the *one* best answer: *a, b, c* or *d*.

1 Howard did not want to lend George the car because   *a)* it was being repaired   *b)* he needed it himself   *c)* George had had an accident before   *d)* George got angry with him.

2 The accident described here happened because   *a)* another car stopped very suddenly   *b)* George tried to overtake   *c)* George was not careful   *d)* he stopped too quickly.

Vocabulary
Find the words that mean   *a)* woman a man intends to marry   *b)* curve in the road   *c)* turn very suddenly   *d)* go sideways and out of control   *e)* part of the car over the engine   *f)* use 'bad', angry language.

Comprehension and interpretation
Explain   *a)* why George wanted to borrow the car   *b)* who Linda was   *c)* where they were going when the accident happened.

Now describe   *a)* where the accident happened   *b)* what George was doing just before it happened   *c)* the driver of the other car and what he was doing before the accident   *d)* the damage to the car   *e)* George and Linda after the accident   *f)* what the other car did after the accident.

Question and answer (Interaction)
You are talking to George about the accident; ask questions (and get answers) beginning   *a)* How...?   *b)* Where...?   *c)* What...?   *d)* Was Linda...?   *e)* Were you...?

Discussion
Describe some of the various ways people cause accidents on the roads.

What do you think Howard will do and say when George tells him about the accident?

Related practice
was/were...ing   had (done)
came/did/smashed, etc.

Study the three examples here

George and Linda **were driving** along a road
They **came** round a bend
The other car **had stopped** in the middle of the road

Now give the correct forms here.
Yesterday I (walk) down a street when I (see) a car at the side of the road. It (crash) into a tree and the driver (lie) on the ground. I (rush) to him and (try) to help. Luckily, he (be) only badly shaken-up and stunned. I (ask) him how the accident (happen). 'Well,' he explained, 'I (drive) home when a child (run) into the middle of the road in front of me. I (swerve) and the car (crash) into that tree.'

Describing an accident
Now describe an accident you have seen yourself or can imagine. Use these points and carefully build your description around them.   *a)* What *were you doing* when you saw the accident or the signs of it?   *b)* What *did you do* then?   *c)* Now describe how the accident *had happened*.

Reporting questions
If you are talking about questions *after you have asked them*, use a form like

What's wrong?
I asked what was wrong

Has there been an accident?
I asked if there had been an accident

How did it happen?
I asked how it had happened

Now report these questions   *a)* Was anybody hurt?   *b)* Whose fault was it?   *c)* Are the police coming?   *d)* Did anybody see the accident?   *e)* Who saw it?   *f)* Where's the driver?

1·1c

Listen to or read the dialogue
It is about half an hour after the accident. George is phoning Howard to tell him.

1

Howard: Hello? Benchley 291989.
George: Is . . . is that you, Howard?
Howard: Who's that? George? Is that you?
George: Yes. Er . . . listen, Howard, I . . . I don't know how to tell you this. I . . . er . . .
Howard: What's wrong? Has something happened?
George: Yes, I . . . I'm a bit shaken-up and I've . . . I've got a nasty cut on my forehead. I . . . I'll pay for the damage, but . . .
Howard: What the devil are you talking about? *(suddenly understanding)* You . . . you're not trying to tell me something has happened to the car, are you?
George: Just give me a chance to explain how it all happened.

2

Howard: How what happened, for God's sake? You haven't told me yet!
George: You see, we skidded off the road and crashed into a fence, but . . .
Howard: Crashed? *(trying to control himself)* Crashed? You mean, you've damaged the car! I'll . . . I'll break your neck, you bloody maniac! You stupid, d . . .
George: Would you let me speak for a moment? I mean, just give me a chance, will you?
Howard: I told you not to take any risks!
George: I didn't take any risks! And it wasn't my fault!

3

Howard: That's what you said last time!
George: (shouting) Are you going to let me explain, or aren't you?
Howard: How bad is the damage?
George: That's what I'm trying to tell you!
Howard: (grimly; calming down) Go on.
George: You see, I was driving along a narrow road and *(fade)* . . .

Exercises
What are the phrases you can use here
a) just before you tell someone some very bad news   b) when someone sounds very confused and you are angry and impatient   c) when you are angry because someone keeps interrupting you and won't let you speak   d) when someone uses an excuse you don't believe because you have heard the same one before from that same person.

Reproduction
The dialogue is divided into three sections. Look at each section separately again. Close your book and see if you can take the role of George. A friend or the teacher will read you Howard's part. Try to remember *more or less* what George says in each part.

Open-ended dialogue
Howard has just put the phone down and is talking to his wife. What do you think he is saying to her?
He: ____
She: What? Oh, no! Not really!
He: ____
She: Try to calm down a bit. It doesn't sound that bad. I mean, the damage can be repaired. What about George?
He: ____
She: Oh, come now! You can't really mean that! After all, he *is* your brother!

Development
Now finish the dialogue between George and Howard. Use these points

George describes the accident.
Howard keeps interrupting and asking about the damage.
George finally describes it.
Howard asks for a description of the other car and the licence number.

Now go on! Do you think George noticed the licence number? What happens now?

1.1d

Further practice

Threats and promises

I'll break your neck!
I'll pay for the damage

Read both sentences aloud, and be careful to make the intonation different.
One sentence is really a threat. The other is a promise. Which is which?

Now read these sentences aloud with what you think is the correct intonation. Also, say whether you think the sentence is a threat or a promise and suggest the situation you might say it in and who you think would use it to whom.

I'll always love you.
I'll kill you if you do that again.
I'll never do that again!
I'll pack my bags and leave if you do!
I'll never come back again.
I'll give up all my bad habits if you stay.

If you are talking about what George and Howard said after they said it, you would probably say

Howard threatened to break George's neck
George promised to pay for the damage

Now transform each statement with either **threatened to ...** or **promised to ...**

George: I'll buy new headlights.
Howard: I'll break your arm!
George: And I'll punch your nose!
Howard: All right. I'll listen carefully!
George: I'll repair the car myself.
Howard: I'll do the same damage to your car!
Howard: I'll smash the headlights and tear the mudguards off!

Look at some other ways of making threats and promises. Which do you think is which?

I'm going to beat the living daylights out of you
You can rely on me to help you
I'll do whatever you want. Don't worry!
Watch it or I'll break your arm off!

Now use one of these various ways to *promise* to a) pay all the repair costs b) put the car back into good order c) clean the floors and cook the meals tomorrow d) work harder e) live a 'clean' life f) stay out of trouble.

Now *threaten* to a) call the police b) break all the windows c) get the Mafia to help you d) cause so much trouble that the whole world will know about it.

Story telling (oral and/or written practice)
You are George. You are sitting in a pub talking about the accident to a friend named Tom.

Describe the accident itself.

Explain why you never got the other car's licence number.

Now tell Tom about the conversation you had on the phone with Howard. (Note: Tom should interrupt and ask questions like 'Why didn't you ...?' 'What happened when ...?' 'Sorry, could you tell me again why/how/what ...?')

Now *write* a letter to another friend explaining why you haven't any money (repair bills for Howard's car) and would like to borrow £300 from him or her.

1·2a 'HARD TIMES'

Look at the picture and discuss

Which man do you think is the other's boss? Give reasons for your answer.

There is a 'sales chart' in the picture. Where? What does it show?

You want more money from your boss. What would you do and say to get it?

Pre-questions for the text

What does one man want from the other?

Why does he want it?

What are some of the other man's problems?

'Unless I get a rise, I'll have to leave,' George Strong said to himself. The morning shift was just beginning and he was sitting at his desk in the design department. George liked his job, the town he lived in, and even his boss, Henry Manley. But his wife kept telling him that she simply could not make ends meet on his salary. That was why he was thinking of taking a job in Birmingham, which was the nearest big city and was about 50 miles away. He had been offered the job in a factory there, and both pay and promotion prospects were far better.

George lived in Wyeford, a medium-sized town with a population of about 65,000. There was a lot of fine countryside and farmland around it. Its main industries were electrical engineering and shoemaking. He really liked the place and was not at all keen on the idea of living or working in Birmingham. However, road and rail connections were very poor. So if he took the job, he would probably have to move his whole family there. It was obviously out of the question for him to work in Birmingham but go on living in Wyeford.

Henry Manley, the manager of Manley Electrics, was going through the accounts that morning. Times were very hard. His small company specialised in manufacturing electric motors. The company was in deep trouble because, among other reasons, the Japanese were selling such things at very low prices. As a result, Manley had had to cut his own prices and profits as well. Otherwise he would not get any orders at all. Even then, orders were still not coming in fast enough, so that there was very little money for investment and none for rises for his workforce. Somehow he had to struggle along, and keep his best men as well. He sighed. Just then the phone rang.

His secretary told him that George Strong wanted to see him about 'something personal' as soon as possible. Manley sighed again. He could guess what it was. Strong was a very good young design engineer. The company had no future unless it could attract and keep men like him. Manley rubbed his forehead. He was desperate. His problems seemed endless. He had to see Strong that morning.

1·2b

Text: comprehension and discussion

Multiple choice comprehension
Choose the *one* best answer: *a, b, c* or *d*.
1 George was thinking of going to Birmingham because *a)* it was a better place   *b)* his family was already there   *c)* pay was better there   *d)* Manley would not give him a rise.
2 Times were hard for Manley because *a)* he had no orders   *b)* his prices were too high   *c)* his best men were leaving him   *d)* he had to sell at very low prices.

Vocabulary
Find the words that mean   *a)* full period of work in a factory   *b)* more pay   *c)* chances of a higher job   *d)* the thing that shows you profits, losses, etc.

Now explain   *a)* make ends meet   *b)* road and rail connections   *c)* he was not keen on the idea   *d)* Manley was desperate.

Comprehension and interpretation
Describe   *a)* George Strong's job   *b)* where he lived and worked   *c)* how he felt about his job   *d)* how he felt about leaving it.

Explain   *a)* what he had decided to do that morning   *b)* why he might have to live in Birmingham   *c)* all the problems Manley had.

What did Manley 'guess' when his secretary told him George wanted to see him?

Why do you think he felt 'desperate'?

Question and answer (Interaction)
You are talking to George before he sees Manley. Ask him questions about   *a)* why he wants to see Manley   *b)* the other job (Where? Why?)   *c)* Wyeford (size, population, main industries, etc.). Be sure to get answers too!

You are talking to Manley before he sees George. Ask questions like   *a)* ... important ... keep ...?   *b)* Why ...?   *c)* ... a rise?   *d)* ... profits?   *e)* Why ..., cutting ... prices?

Discussion
Which seems better? *Give reasons!* A job that is   *a)* well-paid but boring   *b)* not very well-paid but interesting.

Related practice
**... because, among other reasons, ...
As a result, ...   Otherwise, ...
... so that ...**
Study the way these are used in the *third* paragraph (Henry Manley was ... phone rang.) Then use them to connect or relate the sentences below.

George Strong wanted a higher salary. He needed a bigger house. He had a small house with only two bedrooms. He had three children. They all had to sleep in one bedroom. He had to earn more. He could not afford a bigger house. He was going to see Manley. He could explain all this to him.

Now use these words again in explaining   *a)* why you would like to have a car (or a bigger one than the one you have already got)   *b)* why you think (*one reason*) a friend of yours is not learning English very well is that he or she never tries to speak it.

Describing a town or city

Read the description of Wyeford again. Then describe a town or city you know. Use phrases like   *a)* medium-sized/large/small   *b)* population   *c)* main industries   *d)* road and rail connections   *e)* the nearest big city is ...

Certain and uncertain plans

Which of the two sounds less certain?
**I'm going to leave Wyeford
I'm thinking of leaving Wyeford**

Now use the forms to express both certain and uncertain intentions to   *a)* find a new job   *b)* emigrate to Canada   *c)* sell your car   *d)* punch me on the nose   *e)* see a film this evening.

You must have other plans, certain and uncertain! What are they?

1·2c

Listen to or read the dialogue
George Strong has just come into Manley's office.

1

Manley: Sit down, George, won't you?
Strong: Thanks, Mr Manley. It's nice of you to see me.
Manley: Don't mention it, George. I mean, er..., it's the least I can do if you've got ... some sort of problem. *(pause)* Tell me, what can I do for you?
Strong: Well ... I'll come straight to the point. I'm ... I'm thinking of taking a job in Birmingham. It's a question of money, you see. My wife and I ... we can't make ends meet on my salary, if you know what I mean.

2

Manley: (another pause) Ahh, well now. This job in Birmingham. You say you're *thinking* of taking it. Does that mean you're not certain, yet?
Strong: Yes, in a way. I mean, ... I don't really want to leave my job here or Wyeford. But the salary in Birmingham is much better.
Manley: So you're really asking me for a rise? Is that it?
Strong: I ... I'm trying to find out if a rise is possible. Yes.
Manley: Do you mind if I ask how much higher your salary in Birmingham would be?
Strong: About ... £45 a month.

3

Manley: Hmm. Of course you realise ... you'd probably have to buy a house there.
Strong: Yes. Of course.
Manley: House prices there are much higher than here, you know.
Strong: Yes, I've thought of all that. But I'd still move there ... unless I could earn a bit more here.
Manley: Well, now ... er ... let's just talk about this a bit, shall we? You see, the firm at the moment is in rather a difficult ... *(fade)*

Exercises

Find the phrases that you can use
a) to get a person to start talking (who you think wants something from you)
b) when someone thanks you for something   c) when you have something important to say and want to start talking about it immediately
d) when you think you perhaps could have found a better way of saying something but hope you have been understood.

Reproduction
As before, the dialogue is divided into sections 1, 2 and 3. Go through each section separately, with books closed. Take the part of *Strong*. See if you can remember *more or less* what he said. Check each section after you have done it. Look ahead to the next section. Close books again and continue.

Open-ended dialogue
What do you think *Manley* is saying here?
Manley: ___
Strong: Yes, I've heard that things are pretty difficult now. But I still need more money, Mr Manley. I'm sorry.
Manley: ___
Strong: To be honest, at least £35.
Manley: ___
Strong: No, that just isn't enough!
Manley: ___
Strong: But it's still £30 less than what I could earn in Birmingham!

Development
Work out what both people say.

Manley talks about how much better it is to stay in a place like Wyeford. Strong says he still needs a bigger house.
Manley offers £20 a month now and talks about 'better things in the future'.

What happens now? Does Strong accept? Complete the dialogue yourself.

Further practice

Two ways of getting information

Tell me, what can I do for you? Type A
Tell me what I can do for you Type B

Read the two sentences aloud. Make sure you change the pausing and intonation.

There is a difference in structure between the two. What is it?

Which of the two seems more like an order or command?

Read out Type B again with different intonations for these situations *a)* you want to sound very polite *b)* you have very little time to waste and don't like the other person *c)* you are promising someone 'personal' service.

Now transform the questions below in both ways (as above). Be very careful with pausing and intonation, particularly with Type A.

What's wrong?
How much money do you want?
Where is this other job?
What does your wife think about this?
When do you want to leave?

Suppose you are George and you are telling your wife or a friend about what was said at the interview. Notice there is a different way of transforming *a)* real questions *b)* questions that are requests.

Where is the job?
He asked me where the job was

Tell me about it, won't you?
He asked me to tell him about it

Now transform in one way or the other

Why do you want to leave?
Could you tell me the name of the company?
Why don't you think it over?
How soon do you want the rise?
Come and see me tomorrow, won't you?
What kind of holidays will you get?

Awkward questions

Do you mind if I ask how much higher the salary is?

This form is often used to ask rather delicate or 'awkward' questions, when you think it may be too personal to ask directly. Suppose you are talking to George. In the same way ask these questions.

What's the name of the company?
Who's the manager there?
How much money are they offering?
How many hours do you have to work?
Why does your wife want you to apply for it?

Also practise asking such questions with the forms

Would you mind telling me . . . ?
I hope you don't mind me asking . . . ?

Story telling (oral and/or written practice)
Describe what happened that evening when George came home and told Susan, his wife, about the interview with Manley. These notes may help you with the first part of the story.

Susan – window – George came home – car – that evening. She – the door before he – in. 'Well?' she demanded, 'Did you – the rise or didn't you?' George – nothing at first. – very tired. – off his coat – down. ' – a drink first,' he said.

Now finish the story yourself. Did he get the rise or didn't he? Did he decide to stay with Manley? What was Susan's reaction to all this?

1·3a A DANGEROUS PLACE

Look at the picture and discuss

Why do you think the woman is shouting?

Describe the scene as best you can.

Would *you* try to stop the man? Give reasons for your answer.

Pre-questions for the text

Where exactly does the story take place?

Who exactly is 'Paula'?

What is in the black case you see in the man's hand (in the picture)?

Paula had always wanted to go to New York and now she had the chance at last. She was a journalist, and her newspaper was sending her there to do a series of articles on the city. But before she left her home in London, several friends warned her to be careful and not to go out alone at night in New York. 'It's a dangerous place. People get robbed or even killed in broad daylight!' they told her.

But once she got there, the only thing she was ever afraid of was exhaustion. It was so stimulating and exciting a city that she never got any sleep. It took her two weeks to do the articles and she had to interview a lot of people but she enjoyed every minute of it. She completely forgot all her friends' warnings until the day before she went back to London. It all began in a hamburger bar.

She was having lunch there when she suddenly felt someone was watching her. She looked up and noticed a man sitting at a table opposite her. He was staring at her, but looked away. She noticed that he had a scar on his cheek. He was about 30, thick-set and had short, curly hair.

Paula was not worried at all until afterwards. She had to go to an airline office to re-book her flight home. She wanted an afternoon flight instead of a morning one, as originally planned. On her way there, she stopped to look at something in a shop-window. To her surprise she saw the man was following her. She could see his reflection in the glass. He had stopped just behind her. Suddenly she felt afraid. She walked on. Then she stopped and looked behind her again. But this time she could not see him.

Just then she noticed she had come to the airline office. She went in and after she had finished her business, decided to phone a friend from a telephone booth there. She was carrying a small, portable but very expensive tape-recorder. It was in a black case in which she kept her money and passport as well. But the booth was so cramped that she had to leave the case outside. When she came out, it had disappeared. She was stunned. Then she saw the red-haired man hurrying out of the office. He had the case in his hand. She shouted but it was too late.

Text: comprehension and discussion

Multiple choice comprehension
Choose the *one* best answer: *a, b, c* or *d*.
1 When Paula got to New York, she
a) hated it   *b)* loved it   *c)* was always afraid   *d)* heard all sorts of terrible stories.
2 She first noticed the red-haired man
a) outside the airline office   *b)* inside it   *c)* on her way there   *d)* in the hamburger bar.

Vocabulary
Find the words that mean   *a)* tell someone about a danger   *b)* state of being very very tired   *c)* look at in a very obvious way   *d)* can be carried   *e)* very little room to move about in.

Now explain   *a)* She was doing *a series* of articles.   *b)* She saw the man's *reflection*.   *c)* She finished her *business* in the office.

Comprehension and interpretation
Talk about   *a)* Paula's job   *b)* what her friends told her about New York   *c)* what she did in New York, how long she was there and how she felt about it   *d)* what happened the day before she went back to London.

Explain   *a)* where and why she first noticed the man   *b)* exactly what she did from the time she left the hamburger bar to when she came out of the phone booth.

Question and answer (Interaction)
You are a policeman or policewoman and you are talking to Paula a few minutes later. Find out   *a)* who she is (name, nationality, job)   *b)* exactly what was stolen   *c)* how it was stolen   *d)* who she thinks stole it and why?

Then ask a series of questions in order to get as exact a description of the man as possible (How old, etc.).

Discussion
You are in a foreign city. You see a man running towards you. A woman is shouting *what you think* means 'Stop! Murderer!' What would you do? *Give reasons!*

Describe a dangerous city you know. Give warnings to a friend going there.

Related practice

Suddenly . . .   Then . . .
But this time . . .   Just then . . .

Notice how these are used in the last two paragraphs. Then use them below.

Paula was sleeping in her hotel bedroom one night. She heard a bang. She thought she had dreamt it. She heard it again. She lay awake for several minutes, listening. She heard it a third time. There was a scream, as well. She reached for the phone to call the police. The bang came a fourth time and she realised it was someone watching TV in the next room.

Now write a short paragraph yourself with 'Suddenly . . . Then . . . But this time . . . Just then . . .'. The paragraph can be about   *a)* hearing and then seeing a mouse in your bedroom   *b)* mistaking your friend one night for a burglar; etc.

Describing people

Read the description of the red-haired man. Then describe three other people you know.

Key structures and phrases

thick-set/thin/slim/fat/stocky
tall/short/of medium height
fairhaired/dark/balding.

Warnings

Some ways of warning people are

Be sure not to . . .   Be sure to . . .
Don't ever . . .   You must always . . .

How do you think Paula's friends actually warned her   *a)* not to go out alone   *b)* never to leave her door unlocked   *c)* to carry a small revolver   *d)* never to trust strangers   *e)* to take care of her money.

1.3c

Listen to or read the dialogue
Paula is in a police station. She wants to report the theft of her tape-recorder and, more important, her money and passport.

1

Paula: I want to report a theft.
Policeman: A theft?
Paula: Yes. My tape-recorder, my money and ...
Policeman: Sergeant Schwarz, lady.
Paula: Who? What? I mean, wh ...
Policeman: Andy! I got a theft here!
Schwarz: Yeah, yeah! I'm coming!
Policeman: He's coming now, lady.
 (pause)

2

Schwarz: What can I do for you, lady?
Paula: I want to report a theft. My tape-recorder's been stolen and I had everything in ....
Schwarz: Yeah, yeah! Not so fast. I gotta write all this down. Now ... uh ... what was the object?
Paula: Sorry? What was the ... the what?
Schwarz: The object! The thing stolen!
Paula: A tape-recorder and, more important than that, my money and ...
Schwarz: What make, lady?
Paula: It was a Uher. But I'm really ...
Schwarz: What make did you say it was? Spell it!
Paula: (angry) Oh! U ... H ... E ... R.

3

Schwarz: O ... U ... H ... E ... R?
Paula: No! No! Just U ... H ... E ... R! But the ...
Schwarz: Don't shout! Just keep calm! Now, what was its value?
Paula: I don't really know. About £200.
Schwarz: 200 what? What?
Paula: Pounds! English money! But look! I'm far more interested in my passport and money!
Schwarz: What's that got to do with it?
Paula: They've been stolen!
Schwarz: I thought you said your tape-recorder had been stolen!

Exercises

Explain what the first policeman means when he says

Sergeant Schwarz, lady.
Andy! I got a theft here!

Find more polite ways of saying
Yeah, yeah! Not so fast!
What make, lady?
Spell it!
What's that got to do with it?

Paula is often interrupted. What are all the things she would have said if Schwarz had allowed her to finish?

Reproduction

Go through section 1 of the dialogue. Then close your book. A friend or the teacher reads you the role of policeman. Try to remember *more or less* what Paula says.

Then go through sections 2 and 3. This time the friend/teacher should read you the role of Schwarz.

Development

Now finish the dialogue. Another, and more polite policeman, O'Hara, takes over from Schwarz. He asks Paula
a) where the things were stolen   b) to describe the thief   c) if and where she had seen him before   d) the serial number of both the Uher and her passport (she cannot remember either!)   e) if anybody in New York can identify her (she has a friend in New York; an architect named Hugo Wellmeier, 245 West Sutton Place, telephone 567722).

1·3d

Further practice

Repeating questions, pressing for more information

Like Schwarz, you may sometimes ask a question and not really understand the answer. So, for example, instead of simply repeating 'What make was it?' or 'Where did you lose it?' you say

Sorry? What make did you say it was?
Sorry? Where did you say you lost it?

Re-phrase these questions in the same way

How much did it cost?
What was its value?
How do you spell that?
When did you see the man?
What did he look like?
How old was he?
Why did you put your passport in the case?

If a person is very excited and you want to establish a calm atmosphere, you can use a number of forms, like

Perhaps you could tell me again what the man looked like
I wonder if you'd mind telling me again what he looked like
I'd like to ask you just once more what he looked like

Use one of these forms to repeat questions like

What colour hair did he have?
Which hand was the thumb missing from?
Where did you first see him?
Why did you think he was following you?
What did you do when you saw him?
Why did you leave the case outside?

Reporting warnings
rather than actually giving them

Paula is probably saying things to herself like

My friends warned me to be careful
They warned me not to do such things

If you were Paula, how would you talk about these warnings later? Your friends said

Don't ever leave things in front of phone boxes
Always keep your money with you!
Don't go to Irish Dan's on 44th Street
Don't travel on the subway after midnight
Carry a revolver with you!
But don't shoot anybody with it!

Now can you think both of the actual form of warnings and the way you would talk about them later for these situations?

A friend is going for a walk near a farm where you know there is a big and very unfriendly dog.

The same friend is going to try to cheat in an examination. You know he will be watched by a teacher with very sharp eyes.

Another friend has become very interested in a pretty girl. You know that she has a big, brutal and very jealous boyfriend.

Story telling/report writing

You are Paula Robinson and you have to write a short summary of what happened, etc.

Use these points   *a)* Give your name, nationality and occupation   *b)* Give the date of the theft (Nov. 12, 19___) and the whereabouts (Trans Europe Airlines Central Ticket Office, Times Square)   *c)* Describe the things you did just before the theft, exactly what was stolen and all other details you think relevant.

1·4a A QUARREL

Look at the picture and discuss

Why do you think the woman is angry?

What do you think the man and woman are *saying*?

What *excuses* (or lies) do you use when late?

Pre-questions for the text

What is the man's excuse?

What do you think is going to happen just as the story ends?

Mike could see there was going to be trouble. He and his girlfriend, Glenda, had had a bitter quarrel only the week before because he had been late for a dinner-date. He was sure it was going to happen again. He was attending a Teachers' Union meeting at school. It was already 8 o'clock in the evening and he was supposed to meet Glenda at 8.15 in front of a cinema in the centre of town, at least 10 minutes drive away. The meeting, which had been called suddenly that afternoon, was obviously not going to end soon. Since Glenda had no phone, there had been no way of contacting her. 'Oh, my God,' he thought to himself. 'How am I going to get out of this damned thing?' He looked at his watch again and tried to look interested in the discussion about new salary scales.

Glenda got to the cinema just before 8.15. She was a nurse and had to work long hours at the hospital, so she did not like to waste what little free time she had. That was why she always got angry whenever Mike was not punctual. In the six months they had been going out together, he had been late time and time again. Even worse, he always had some silly excuse which she could hardly believe. 'He'd better be on time this evening, or else!' she thought.

Mike was getting more and more impatient. At 8.05 he suddenly stood up. He felt terribly embarrassed. They were still arguing about salaries. 'I'm terribly sorry but I've got an appointment,' he said. Everybody stared. He stumbled over their feet, cursing to himself. Then he grabbed his coat, dashed to his car, and drove away. Then things really became difficult. First of all, traffic was very heavy and the main roads were jammed. To make matters worse, the cinema was up a one-way street. But worst of all, there was nowhere to park. He got so desperate that he left the car in a no-parking zone. It was past 8.30 when he got to the cinema. Glenda was waiting there. Her eyes were blazing with anger.

1.4b

Text: comprehension and discussion

Vocabulary
Find the word or phrase that means *a)* angry conversation between two or more people *b)* on time, not late *c)* system of different levels of pay for teachers, doctors, etc. *d)* feel nervous, out of place *e)* almost fall *f)* blocked with traffic.

Explain the phrases *a)* He was *attending* a meeting. *b)* He had a *dinner-date*. *c)* He went up a *one-way* street. *d)* He left the car in a *no-parking zone*. *e)* Her eyes were *blazing* with anger.

Question and answer (Interaction)
You are a friend of Mike's. He is telling you about his date with Glenda the next day. Find out *a)* when he was supposed to meet Glenda *b)* where he was just before he met her *c)* why he didn't tell her about the meeting *d)* if he was very worried at the meeting and why *e)* what he finally did in order to get out *f)* what sort of trouble he had then (traffic, etc.). Get answers!

Now imagine you are talking to Glenda about her date last night. What sort of questions can you ask her?

Discussion and interpretation
Imagine the sorts of things Glenda will do and say when Mike tries to explain why he is late. Work out their conversation.

After a quarrel such as Glenda and Mike have, which do you think is the best thing to do? Again, give reasons. *a)* try to forget it as soon as possible *b)* be cold and distant for a few days just to show the other person that he/she 'can't get away with it again'.

Related practice

was going to . . .
had (done/been, etc.)   was . . . ing

Examine the way these forms are used in the text. Then use them here.

Glenda (wait) in front of the cinema when Mike got there. He (be) late only the week before. As soon as he saw her face, he knew they (have) another quarrel. At the same time he (think) about his car. He (leave) it in a no-parking zone and he was sure he (get) a parking-ticket.

Apologising
Here are 3 ways of apologising

I should like to apologise for having been late
Sorry I was (or I'm) late
I hope you'll excuse me for being late.

Now say which you would *most probably* use with *a)* a friend you know really well *b)* someone you are on formal terms with (boss, headmaster, etc.) and are *speaking* to *c)* someone like *b)* you are *writing* to.

Now apologise to *each of the three* people for *a)* not coming to an important meeting yesterday *b)* spilling coffee all over the floor *c)* quarrelling with their husband or wife.

Describing difficulties
Look at the description of Mike's difficulties in getting to the cinema. Note how phrases like

First of all
To make matters worse
But worst of all

are used to relate the sentences to each other.

Now write a similar short description of your difficulties in *a)* getting to work or school one day *b)* finding a hotel room in a strange city *c)* falling asleep one night.

1·4c Listen to or read the dialogue

1

Mike has just got to the cinema.

Mike: (*out of breath*) Gl... Glenda. Sorry I'm late but I...
Glenda: (*coldly*) So there you are. (*pause*) Well, what's your excuse this time?
Mike: I'm sorry, but it wasn't my fault. I... where're you going? (*He runs after her*) Give me a chance to explain, will you? Listen! Please!
Glenda: To what? To another of your stupid excuses? It's too late for the film now. You just don't give a damn, do you?
Mike: Of course I do! Look, are you going to stop and listen to me or aren't you?

2

Glenda: Stop shouting! People are looking at you!
Mike: But you won't let me explain.
Glenda: (*stopping now*) Why don't you at least try to be punctual? You just...
Mike: But I do try! And I did try this evening!
Glenda: I suppose your car broke down again, or something like that?
Mike: No, of course not. The union called a meeting suddenly this evening. It was supposed to end around 8 but it didn't.

3

Glenda: Oh, why do you have to tell such... such stupid lies? You must think I'm a fool!
Mike: Of course I don't think you're a fool! And I'm *not* lying, damn it!
Glenda: Go on! Swear! Make a big scene right here in the street!
Mike: But you've just accused me of lying! *I'm* not making the scene!
Glenda: Well, I'm going home if you can't even control yourself!
Mike: But, damn it, oh... look. I'm sorry. Why don't we... I mean, can't we... er... Let's have a drink somewhere and I'll explain.

Exercises

How exactly does Glenda say that *a*) she is sure he hasn't got a good excuse *b*) he really is not sorry in the least *c*) he never even tries to come on time *d*) the excuse he gave last time was a very bad one and he had better not use the same one again *e*) the excuse he is giving now is like all the others: a lie *f*) he ought to stop swearing and making a scene.

And how does Mike say that *a*) he is really going to get angry if she doesn't listen to him *b*) what she says about him not trying, etc., simply isn't true *c*) it is she, and not he, who is causing the scene.

Open-ended dialogue
What do you think Glenda is saying here?

Mike: I didn't know about the meeting before it was called.
Glenda: ____
Mike: But I didn't, I tell you! And I've never used a teachers' meeting as an excuse before!
Glenda: ____
Mike: But I *did* leave before it was over. It's going on now!
Glenda: ____
Mike: No, that wasn't a lie, either! It actually *did* break down!

Development
Finish the dialogue yourself. Mike explains *a*) why he could not tell her he might be late *b*) how he rushed out of the meeting *c*) his parking problems, etc.
What do you think happens then?

1·4d

Further practice

Accusations

You are Mike. You are telling a friend what happened between you and Glenda last night. Her actual words were 'You just don't give a damn, do you?' and 'Why do you have to tell such stupid lies?'

In talking about this later, you can say

She accused me of not giving a damn
She accused me of lying

Report these things in the same way.
You always come late
You just don't care, do you?
Why can't you be honest with me?
You started the quarrel!
You have another girl friend, haven't you?
You didn't even try to be punctual!

Look again at the dialogue and the various ways Glenda accuses Mike of things. How, for example, does she accuse him of   a) thinking she is a fool   b) not trying to be punctual   c) making a scene.

Now read out these sentences. Make them sound like accusations.

Why can't you be honest?
Why are you lying to me?
Why don't you tell the truth?

You are Mike. Use one of the forms you have seen here (or others you can think of) to accuse Glenda of   a) not giving you a chance to explain   b) not listening to you   c) losing her temper   d) making life impossible for you   e) not trusting you.

Denials

Mike *denies* a number of things. For example, what is he denying when he says

Of course I do!
But I do try! And I did try this evening!
I'm not lying, damn it!
I'm not making the scene!

Imagine you have been in a car accident. How would you deny these things? The other driver is saying

You caused the accident!
You're drunk!
You stopped in the middle of the road!
You tried to overtake when it was dangerous!
You can't drive properly!
You haven't even got a driving licence!

If Mike reports some of his denials to a friend (after the quarrel), he will probably say things like

I denied that I was lying
I denied having lied before!

Now look again at the statements above (car accident). How would you report those denials to a friend after you had made them?

Suggestions

Mike suggests having a drink. He can say

Why don't we have a drink?
Can't we have a drink?
Let's have a drink
Wouldn't it be a good idea to have a drink?

Now suggest   a) going to another film   b) talking calmly   c) seeing the film tomorrow   d) going to a night club   e) sitting down somewhere   f) talking about it later.

Letter writing

Glenda got angry and went home. The next day Mike writes to her. How do you think he   a) apologises again for last night   b) explains fully what happened and why he was late   c) suggests meeting again or coming to her place next Saturday?

Write this out first as a short letter. Then imagine the same content in a *phone conversation* between Mike and Glenda. Imagine what Glenda says, as well.

18

1.5a The Opinion Survey

Look at the picture and discuss

The woman in the picture is doing something called 'market research'. Try to explain what this is.

What kind of questions do you think she is asking?

Pre-questions for the text

Give at least one reason the woman has decided to do such work.

Does it seem from the story that she is doing the job very well?

Carol was slowly going out of her mind with boredom. After ten years of being a housewife and a mother, she could not stand it any longer. Then, one morning, just after her two daughters had gone to school, she saw an advertisement in the paper. She phoned, and was asked to come to an interview that very afternoon.

**Market Research Agency seeks
OPINION SURVEYORS**

Part-time (9.30–1.30, 5 days a week). Good pay and conditions. The job involves gathering information about shopping habits and trends. Ideal for well-educated housewives, 21–45. Apply by letter, Mr K. Hollins, 12 Rupert Street, or phone 290345, 8.30–5, Mon. to Fri.

Mr Hollins turned out to be a young man about 24 in a natty blue suit. There was a hard look in his eye and he talked very fast. He told her she would be required to stop men between the ages of 21 and 50 and interview them. Each interview consisted of a series of questions designed to determine men's attitudes to deodorants. The information was to be recorded on special questionnaires and she would be paid according to the number of complete interviews she obtained.

When Carol asked which manufacturer the research was for, she was told that did not really concern her. Last of all, before she began she would have to attend a one-day training-session. Carol accepted.

After the training-session, which was really only about how to fill in the questionnaires correctly and how to put the questions themselves, Carol found herself in the centre of town at 9.30 in the morning. She soon found out that getting the information was really not all that easy.

First, she stopped a man who refused to answer any questions because he had no time. Next, a man told her it was none of her business if he used deodorants. Then she interviewed a man who was hard of hearing and instead of answering her questions, began asking her all sorts of his own. Finally, Carol spotted a young man with a pleasant smile on his face. He was coming towards her slowly and seemed ready to talk. He looked startled when she put her first question. 'I'm doing an opinion survey, too. It's about soap powders,' he said.

Text: comprehension and discussion

Vocabulary
Find the word or phrase that means *a)* smart, neat (for clothes)   *b)* find out about   *c)* feelings, opinion about   *d)* something that stops or hides bad smells   *e)* form full of questions   *f)* somebody who makes things   *g)* surprised.

Now explain the meaning of   *a)* She was *going out of her mind with boredom*.   *b)* She could not *stand it* any longer.   *c)* She had to ask questions about their *shopping-habits*.   *d)* She would be paid *according to* the number of interviews she obtained.   *e)* One man told her it was *none of her business*.   *f)* Another man was *hard of hearing*.

Question and answer (Interaction)
You are talking to Mr Hollins about the job advertised in the paper, but you have not seen the advertisement. Find out about   *a)* the work itself   *b)* hours   *c)* how you will be paid   *d)* who can apply for it.

Now you are talking to Carol immediately after the interview. Ask her   *a)* why she wants the job   *b)* how she found out about it   *c)* what she did then   *d)* to describe the man who interviewed her   *e)* what she has to do in the job   *f)* if she knows who the research is for (Why not?).

Now you are talking to her after her first morning. What questions can you ask her to find out what happened (the four men, etc.)?

Discussion and interpretation
Why do you think the last young man was 'coming towards her slowly' and 'seemed ready to talk'? Give reasons.

You apply for a job as an 'international messenger', carrying 'parcels' to various countries. You are interviewed above a shabby garage in a back street. The pay is extremely high. You are told never to look into the parcels, and that the name of your employer is 'none of your business'. Would you accept the job? Again, *give reasons*.

Related practice

First Next Then Finally

Note how these are used in the last paragraph. Then use them yourself to describe   *a)* what you usually do immediately after you get up in the morning   *b)* how you operate a simple machine, like a tape-recorder, coffee-grinder or record-player (or how you start a car)   *c)* how coffee or tea is made in your country.

Describing a job

Look at the advertisement again and then the other information about the job in the second paragraph.

Then describe other jobs you know of (shop-assistant, factory worker, teacher, etc.). Use terms like

Part-time, full-time,
the job involves . . . ing,
paid according to . . . ,
the hours are from . . . o'clock to . . . ,
Monday to . . . etc.

Instructions

One formal way of giving instructions, particularly in writing, is this construction:

The information is **to be recorded** on questionnaires. You **are to start** at 9.

Now, in the same way, give a *series* of instructions for   *a)* a group of school children who have to catch a bus at . . . , wear . . . , and have . . . money with them for a museum visit   *b)* students taking an English exam tomorrow.

1·5c

Listen to or read the dialogue
Carol is interviewing a man. He is rather hard of hearing.

1

Carol: Excuse me, sir. Would you be good enough to answer a few questions for an opinion survey we're doing?
Man: Sorry? What? Would I . . . what?
Carol: (slowly, distinctly) Would you mind helping me with an opinion survey?
Man: An opinion what?
Carol: An opinion survey, sir. I'd like to ask you some questions.
Man: Oh, you want me to answer questions. All right.

2

Carol: Now, first of all, I've got four age groups on this questionnaire here. May I ask you which you're in?
Man: Sorry. I don't quite understand. Which what am I in?
Carol: Age group, sir. Do you see? 18 to 21. 22 to 30. 31 to 39. 40 to 50.
Man: Oh, you want to know how old I am!
Carol: Yes, sir. Exactly.
Man: Oh, well, I'm . . . er . . . er . . . tell me. Why are you asking such questions? I mean, why do you want to know?

3

Carol: Well . . . we're doing some market research for a company that makes deodorants for men, and they . . .
Man: What kind of research? For a company that makes . . . what?
Carol: Market research. And the company makes deodorants. For men.
Man: Good Lord! What are they?
Carol: Well, well they're . . . how shall I explain . . .
Man: Do you mind if I ask *you* something?
Carol: (confused) No. I mean, yes. Oh, go on.
Man: What's a nice girl like you doing this strange kind of work for?
Carol: Well, sir . . . I really haven't time to . . . I mean, . . . *I'm* supposed to ask *you* the questions. So, if you don't mind, could you just tell me which . . . which age group you're in, and then I'd like to know which . . . *(fade)*

Exercises

Close your book and take the role of either Carol or the Man. Go through the three sections of the dialogue with someone else, one by one. (Stop and look over section 2 and section 3 again before going on.)

Modification
First orally and then in writing, rework the dialogue based on these points   *a)* The man is not hard of hearing, understands all the questions, and does not ask Carol any about herself.   *b)* He is 47, and owns a pet shop.   *c)* He never uses deodorants. His wife bought him one once. He threw it away.

Reproduction
Here is another interview. What do you think Carol is saying?

Carol: ___
Man: No, go ahead, but I really haven't got much time.
Carol: ___
Man: No, of course I don't mind. I'm in the second one, 22 to 30.
Carol: ___
Man: Yes, I do. But only in hot weather. In the summer, mostly.
Carol: ___
Man: No, not myself. My girlfriend gets them for me.
Carol: ___
Man: No, I'm afraid I can't remember which brands or anything like that.

Development
Work out another interview with a man of 35 who is shocked by the question and thinks such research ought not to be done.

1·5d

Further practice

Questions you don't really understand

It often happens that because of noise, fast speech or other reasons you do not understand a particular word in a question. Here, the word *shambag* (a nonsense word) will stand for the 'unclear' word. Get people to repeat the question like this

Question: Do you ever use shambags?
You: Do I ever use WHAT?
Question: Would you please shambag a moment.
You: Would I WHAT?

Get people to repeat these questions

Have you ever shambagged in your life?
What have you got against shambagging?
Is that a shambag?
Did you know that shambagging is a serious crime in Britain?
Stop shambagging immediately!
Which shambag are you in, sir?
We're doing a market shambag.

More ways of asking 'delicate' questions and making requests

In 1.2d you learned forms like

Do you mind if I ask . . .
Would you mind telling me . . .

Now you have learned more such forms, like

Would you be good enough to . . .
I'd like to ask you . . .
May I ask you . . .
If you don't mind, could you just tell me . . .

Note again the change in structure

How old are you?
May I ask you how old you are?
What do you do?
I'd like to ask you what you do.

Use *various* forms to ask *a)* What's your name? *b)* Do you use deodorants? *c)* Which brands do you use? *d)* Do you buy them yourself? *e)* How much do they cost *f)* Why don't you use them?

Extension work
Think of more questions you might ask with such forms if you were *a)* doing an opinion survey with women from 21 to 35 in which you had to ask them how much they weigh, if they are married, which slimming breakfast foods they use (if any) *b)* asking the director of a language school about fees, number of students in a class, teacher-qualifications, etc.

Reporting refusals

Compare the actual words of refusal and the way Carol talks about them later.

I haven't got any time
One man refused to answer because he said he hadn't any time

I never answer such questions
Another one refused because he said he never answered such questions

You are Carol. Tell someone else about people's refusals in the same way. They said things like

I'm in a hurry!
It's none of your damned business!
I never talk to strangers on the street!
I'm doing an opinion survey myself so I can't help you
Sorry, I'd like to but I have to get to work.

Letter writing
You are Carol Allen. Write a short letter to Mr Hollins (see advertisement for address in Bristol). Tell him *a)* you wish to give up the work *b)* about what happened on your first morning *c)* that you managed to get two interviews in the afternoon *d)* that you are enclosing the completed questionnaires.

Then ask him to send you your money (£4.40) to your address at 12 Carey Road, Bristol.

1·6a A WONDERFUL CHANCE

Look at the picture and discuss

Say why you think or *do not* think these people are a) man and wife b) father and daughter c) boss and employee.

Look at the expressions on both their faces. What do they tell you about the two people's feelings at the moment?

Pre-questions for the text

At the very beginning of the story Janet has got to tell her father something. What?

How does her father feel about it, and why?

Janet knew she would have to tell her father. She dreaded it. 'You'd better tell him this evening. But he won't like the idea at all!' her mother said. They were standing in the small kitchen of the small house where Janet had lived all her life.

Janet was nineteen and a student of Layout and Graphic Design at the local Art College. She had one more year to do in the course. Her father and she had often quarrelled about whether it was the right thing for her to do at all. He did not think she would really be able to get a 'proper job' at the end of it. But he was willing to let her go on as long as she did not 'fool around too much' while she was doing it. And that was the trouble. She had just been given a wonderful chance to go on a one-month tour of Holland and Northern Germany with a small folk music group she often sang with at the College. They would even earn a bit of money! However, it would mean interrupting her studies for a few weeks since the tour was more or less at the beginning of the winter term. She stared out at the gloomy street. Just then she saw her father's car stopping in front of the house. She could see his face in the glare of the streetlamp as he got out and came up the path towards the house. He looked tired and in rather a bad mood.

Janet's father was a foreman in a factory. Although the job was hard and boring, he never complained. For one thing it was secure. For another, the pay was good. Besides, he could remember his own childhood when his father had often been out of work. He came into the front room as usual, that evening, and sat down to watch the news on TV before dinner. Janet brought him a cup of tea, and then told him about the tour.

Janet could see from the angry look on his face that he was seething inside. But she went on talking, and at first he said nothing. Then he told her it was out of the question. It was clear he thought he could forbid her to go. But Janet had already made up her mind that she was going to force him to discuss it with her. She could see it was not going to be easy.

Text: comprehension and discussion

Multiple choice comprehension
Choose the one best answer: *a, b, c* or *d*.

1 Janet dreaded telling her father that she *a)* was studying Graphic Design *b)* had quarrelled with her mother *c)* wanted to go on the tour *d)* was singing with a folk music group.

2 She was afraid to tell him because he *a)* would probably think she was wasting time *b)* had quarrelled with her about the tour *c)* was in a bad mood *d)* was out of work.

3 When she told him, he *a)* said nothing at all *b)* forced her to discuss it with him *c)* said it was not going to be easy *d)* told her she could not go.

Vocabulary
Find the word or phrase that means *a)* be very afraid of *b)* waste time with foolish things *c)* trip, visiting several places *d)* dark and depressing *e)* say that you are unhappy about something *f)* order someone not to do something.

Now explain *a)* He wanted her to get a *proper job*. *b)* It would *mean* interrupting her studies. *c)* His job was *secure*. *d)* He was *seething*.

Question and answer (Interaction)
You and Janet are talking *before* she tells her father. Ask about the tour. For example *a)* How long...? *b)* Which countries...? *c)* What kind of music ...? *d)* ...interrupt your studies?

Now explain to someone else *a)* what Janet was studying *b)* what she and her father had quarrelled about before *c)* how he felt about her studies *d)* why she dreaded telling him about the tour *e)* what kind of work he did *f)* what happened when Janet told him.

Discussion and interpretation
Read again about the childhood and job of Janet's father. Do you think this helps explain his attitude to Janet's studies? If so, say how and why.

If you were Janet would you *a)* go on the tour and risk failing your exams; or *b)* forget the tour and hope for another chance some other time? *Give reasons.*

Related practice

**Although... For one thing, ...
For another, ... Besides, ...**

Study the use of these in the third paragraph.

Janet liked her father. She did not get on very well with him. He was not very open-minded. They had very different ideas about things like sex and politics. They often quarrelled.

Now use them again in a short description of *a)* why you are not happy in a well-paying job (not interesting/long hours/want to leave) *b)* why you will never go to a particular place on holiday again (very beautiful/very unhappy last time, very expensive, food very poor, never go again).

Describing a course of study, etc.

Read this short description. Note the words and phrases in italics.

Janet is *doing* a two-year course *in* Design. It *includes* such things as Layout, Printing Techniques and Technology, and Art Work. At *the end of it*, she will *take* a series of examinations. If she *passes* them and *gets* her diploma, she *hopes to work* in advertising or in book publishing.

Now use such terms to describe *a)* your own English programme *b)* a course you did or are doing in a school or university, etc.

1·6c

Listen to or read the dialogue
Janet has just told her father about the tour.

1

Janet: Well, dad? Don't you think it's a wonderful chance? *(pause)* I mean, I've never been to Germany or Holland!
Her Father: *(pause)* Go on a tour? You mean, sing in ... night clubs and places like that?
Janet: Yes, well that's part of it, but ...
Her Father: And when's this ... tour ... supposed to start, then?
Janet: Next month. After Christmas. First we'll go to Amsterdam, and then to Utrecht. After that, Hanover and ...

2

Her Father: *(suddenly)* No! It's a mad idea.
Janet: *(pause)* Well, I'm sorry you feel that way about it, but I still think we ought to discuss it.
Her Father: You'd have to interrupt your studies, wouldn't you? Eh? Am I right?
Janet: Yes, of course. But it would be only for a little while ...
Her Father: It's out of the question! You can't go! So forget it!
Janet: It sounds almost as if you're forbidding me to go, dad.
Her Father: All right, if you want to put it that way! I forbid you to go!

3

Janet: I'm sorry, dad, but you can't do that! It's for me to decide.
Her Father: Oh, I see. You've already decided, have you? Now you listen to me! You're only 19 ...
Janet: I didn't say I'd already decided, dad! I said it was for me to decide! There's a difference!
Her Father: Oh, so you think you can just do whatever you want, do you?
Janet: I didn't say that, either. I was hoping we could *discuss* the matter together. I want your advice. But I don't want you to tell me what to do! I've got to make decisions for myself, dad ... *(fade)*

Exercises

There is a misunderstanding here. What is it and whose fault do you think it is?

Explain the difference between 'It's for me to decide' and 'I've already decided'.

With books closed, take the role of Janet and try to remember more or less what she says in response to her father. Go through section 1 first, then section 2, etc.

Modification
First orally, and then in writing re-work the dialogue based on these points   *a)* Janet is not talking to her father but to a good friend called Jim.   *b)* Jim is very happy when he hears about the tour. He thinks it is a very good idea.   *c)* Janet at first does not seem very sure about whether to go or not. Jim tells her she ought to, and not be too worried about interrupting her studies.

Development
Finish the dialogue between Janet and her father, based on these points *a)* Janet's father apologises for losing his temper but still thinks she ought to forget the idea.   *b)* Janet points out that she will miss only a week of the winter term since the tour begins at the start of the Christmas holidays (which last three weeks).

Then work out the ending yourself. Does this change her father's attitude? What do you think?

Open-ended dialogue
What do you think Janet's father is saying?
Her Father: ___
Janet: But didn't you understand me? I'll miss only one week, not four!
Her Father: ___
Janet: But that isn't true, dad! Nothing important ever happens that first week!

1·6d

Further practice

Orders and advice

Which of these statements seem like *orders*, and which like *advice*?

Don't go on the tour!
If I were you, I wouldn't go on the tour
I think you'd better finish your studies first
Finish your studies first!

Now change these statements so that instead of telling or ordering a person to do something, they seem like advice or suggestions. Use 'If I were you, I'd . . .', or 'Don't you think you'd better . . .?' or some other *suitable* form you can think of.

Put that cigar out!
Stop smoking so much!
Concentrate on your studies!
Forget the idea!
Go on the tour some other time!
Don't go now!

Now think of polite advice and exactly what you would say in giving it for these situations   a) Paula in *A Dangerous Place* who carries her money about in the tape-recorder case.
b) George Strong in *Hard Times* who has left his job with Manley Electrics but hates his new job and the city he has to live in.   c) Howard, George's brother in *Smash-Up*, who has just been asked by Peter to lend him his car again.   d) Mike in *A Quarrel* who has another date with Glenda this evening. The date is at 8.20. It is 8.15 and he has not left yet.   e) Janet's father, who has just told you he is going to forbid her to go on the tour.

Reporting orders and advice

You overheard the conversation between Janet and her father. Tell someone else what he said. Use either: 'He advised her to/not to . . .', 'He told her to/not to . . .' or 'He forbade her to . . .'.

I'd finish my studies first, if I were you
I mean, I wouldn't go if I were you
You can't go! Understand?
Stop wasting your time at College!
And don't spend any more time with that folk group!
I'm sorry. I should have said 'I really think you'd better not spend any more time with the group!'
Don't you think you ought to talk to your teachers about the idea, too?

Rejecting advice

This is from a later stage of Janet's conversation with her father.

Her Father: So you see, Janet, if I were you, I wouldn't go on the tour!
Janet: Hmm. Wouldn't you? Well, I think I really ought to. But I'll think about what you said just the same.

Use a 'tag' like: 'Wouldn't you?', 'Should I?', 'Do you?' or some other suitable tag, and then add something to reject advice like

I wouldn't drink any more if I were you!
But you've already had too much!
I think you ought to go home now!
You shouldn't drink at all in your state!
You'd really better stop!

Description/letter writing

Describe a tour like Janet's or a tour you yourself have made of a foreign country. This can be in the form of a letter *written in the middle of the tour*. Use such key structures and phrases as

The first day we went to/visited . . .
Then we went on to . . . where we . . .
After that we . . .
We also . . .
Since then we have been . . .

Add details about the weather, night life, what you did and saw, the food, etc.

1.7a A Bad Way to Begin a Marriage

Look at the picture and discuss

What time of the year do you think it is? Why?

What sort of place does this appear to be?

Would you like to spend your holiday here, in such weather? *Give reasons.*

Pre-questions for the text

The two people in the picture are in a town. What is its name and why are they there?

They have a number of reasons to be unhappy. Describe some of them.

'I never thought it was going to be like this,' John said. He was talking about his honeymoon and he looked very disappointed. He and Anna, his bride, were walking along the beach. It was drizzling and a strong wind was blowing. Although it was the middle of summer, it seemed like late autumn.

Everything was wrong. First of all, Bascome, the town they had come to, was not at all like the description they had read in the holiday brochure. It was an ugly seaside town on the East Coast. The beach was full of litter. The cafés and pubs in the town itself were all in the worst sort of 'modern' style, with loud juke boxes and plastic flowers. Secondly, the weather had been dreadful all the five days they had been there. Thirdly, the hotel they were staying at was awful and in addition the food was disgusting. Their room was small, dark and cramped. The bed creaked loudly every time they moved. Breakfast was a greasy fried egg and one thin slice of toast. Dinner was even worse; the meat was always tough and tasteless and the vegetables were overcooked and watery. Last but not least, the hotel was managed by a stout and terrifying lady with the voice and appearance of an army sergeant. Nobody ever dared complain to her. John and Anna had booked for two weeks.

On the sixth day they went for a long walk along the coast. At first, the sky was overcast as usual. But after a while it began to brighten up. The clouds cleared and suddenly the sun came out. About lunchtime they got to a small, very pleasant fishing village. There was a good old-fashioned pub on the quayside. It had a fine view of the harbour. They had some good beer and sandwiches there for lunch. They began to cheer up and started talking to the friendly landlord. Then they sat for a time outside the pub in the warm sunlight and watched the fishing boats sail past them. Suddenly Anna noticed a sign in the pub window. 'Bed and Breakfast. Reasonable Prices'. Then she said 'Why don't we spend the second week here instead of that ghastly hotel in Bascome?'

John began to think of excuses he could use with the terrifying woman back at the hotel. What, he wondered, would she do if he told her they were leaving early?

Text: comprehension and discussion

Multiple choice comprehension
Choose the *one* best answer: *a, b, c* or *d*.

1 Bascome was . . . like the description in the holiday brochure.   *a)* nothing   *b)* exactly   *c)* only a bit   *d)* more or less.

2 John and Anna went to a fishing village and   *a)* found a room there   *b)* decided they could not stay   *c)* had to leave early   *d)* wanted to spend the second week there.

Vocabulary
Find the words that mean   *a)* newly-married wife   *b)* things thrown on the ground and left lying there   *c)* so bad that it makes you sick to look at it   *d)* covered with cloud   *e)* part of the harbour where ships load and unload.

Comprehension and interpretation
Describe   *a)* how John felt about Bascome and why   *b)* the town itself   *c)* the hotel he and Anna were staying at   *d)* the food   *e)* the woman who managed it   *f)* the weather the first five days   *g)* what John and Anna did on the sixth day.

Explain   *a)* why they wanted to stay in the fishing village   *b)* why John began to think of excuses at the end.

Question and answer (Interaction)
You are John's friend and are phoning him on the fifth day. What are your questions about   *a)* the weather so far   *b)* the hotel   *c)* the food   *d)* what they plan to do tomorrow.

Now you are phoning on the sixth day, in the evening. They are back at the hotel in Bascome. Find out   *a)* about the weather today   *b)* what they did in the morning and the afternoon   *c)* what they want to do now   *d)* why.

Discussion
Think of some excuses John might use with the woman at the hotel to explain why he wants to leave suddenly.

Have you ever had a disappointing holiday? Describe it.

Related practice

**First of all, . . . Secondly, . . .
Thirdly, . . . Fourthly, . . .
In addition, . . . Last but not least, . . .**

Use these terms yourself in a short description consisting of *two* of the following things   *a)* why you do or do not want to get married at the present time   *b)* why you would or would not consider taking a particular job, *such as* street sweeper, professional assassin, head lion tamer in a circus, manager of a hotel like the one described in *1.7a*.

Describing the weather

Look at the terms used to describe the weather in the story. Write all of them down. Here are some more.

**It rained heavily
It rained off and on throughout the day
It was hot and humid
It was freezing
It got/became dark and overcast
There was thunder and lightning
It snowed
It was cold and damp
We had fog/mist
The weather was clear/fine/very dry**.

Now use them to describe the changes in weather where you live. Begin *'Last week'* or *'A few days ago.'*

Excuses

**I'm awfully sorry but I've simply got to . . .
I hope you won't mind but I . . .
I'm sorry but I can't/I haven't . . .**

Use one or more of these forms as an excuse for   *a)* not coming to the party this evening   *b)* changing a dinner date   *c)* leaving the party early   *d)* not coming to a lesson   *e)* not doing the homework   *f)* not coming to the big test tomorrow.

1.7c

Listen to or read the dialogue
John and Anna have decided to spend the second week of their honeymoon in the fishing village. John is going to tell Miss Fox.

1

John: (nervously) Miss Fox. I . . . I . . . wonder if I could speak to you for a moment.
Fox: (barking) I'm busy! Can't it wait?
John: Well . . . I'm sorry to disturb you, but it's important. I mean, er . . . I've got to tell you now.
Fox: Tell me? Tell me what?
John: About next week. I mean, er . . . my wife and I have got to leave tomorrow.

2

Fox: Tomorrow? But that's only the end of the first week. You've booked for two.
John: Yes, I know. I mean, er . . . that's what I'm trying to explain. We can't stay for the two weeks. You see . . . it's my mother-in-law. You know. My wife's mother.
Fox: (suspiciously) Your mother-in-law?
John: Yes, she's, er . . . she's fallen ill. She's in hospital and . . . and we've got to go back.
Fox: I see. And?
John: And . . . er . . . and . . . we can't stay the second week! As I've just told you! (firmly) So I'd like to settle the bill now, please.

3

Fox: Settle the bill? Pay?
John: Yes, exactly. We're leaving very early in the morning!
Fox: Very well. (opens account book, adds a few figures on the machine) £30 per person for the first week. That's £60. And then 10 per cent cancellation fee.
John: Ten per cent cancellation what?
Fox: Just a moment, please. That'll be £66 altogether, please.
John: What's the extra £6 for?
Fox: Cancellation fee. You booked for two weeks! I've reserved the room for you!
John: But . . . but we're not going to use it the second week.
Fox: I'm very sorry but you'll have to pay the cancellation fee. (Threateningly) I could charge you for the whole of next week, you know!

Exercises

Explain   *a)* a mother-in-law   *b)* a cancellation fee   *c)* *it* in: *John:* I'm sorry to disturb you but it's important.   *d)* *it* in: *John:* You see . . . it's my mother-in-law.   *e)* *And?* in: *Fox:* I see. And?

Development
Finish the dialogue between John and Miss Fox, based on these points
a) John refuses to pay the cancellation fee.   *b)* Miss Fox says it is a 'standard practice' in the hotel business to charge such things.   *c)* John says he has never heard of such a thing.   *d)* Miss Fox shows him some very small print in the booking form he signed. It mentions the 10 per cent cancellation fee.

Now finish the dialogue yourself. What do you think happens now?

Modification
Re-work the dialogue first orally and then in writing based on these points.
a) The manager's name is Miss Allen. She is extremely polite and kind.
b) John really does have to leave a week earlier than planned. His own father is very ill in hospital.   *c)* When John asks for the bill, she mentions a £2 cancellation fee. But she decides not to charge it because of the circumstances.

1·7d

Further practice

Open-ended dialogue
What is Miss Fox saying?
Fox: ___
John: I don't care if all hotels do it!
Fox: ___
John: Booking form? What booking form?
Fox: ___
John: But I booked by letter.
Fox: ___
John: Yes, of course I remember signing something when we came here.
Fox: ___
John: Does it? Well, I never noticed it!
Fox: ___
John: But it's such small print I can hardly read it! That's not fair.

'Giving in' unwillingly

Sometimes you don't want to do something but you see that you have to, even though you think it is unfair. When he finally pays the cancellation fee, John might say something like

I still don't see why I should have to pay this ridiculous fee, but I'll do so
I'll pay this fee but only under protest
I think it's very unfair that I've got to pay this fee. But I suppose I can't do anything about it

And now, use one of these forms to agree unwillingly to the following things   a) paying a parking fine   b) doing a test   c) leaving your passport with the hotel manager   d) going to a party tomorrow   e) answering 'personal questions' on a questionnaire   f) paying for something in cash and not by cheque.

Obligations, duties, responsibilities

Miss Fox, in pointing out John's obligation, simply said

I'm sorry but you'll have to pay a cancellation fee

She could also have said something like

You do realise that you've got to pay a cancellation fee, don't you?

Use one of these forms, beginning with 'I'm sorry but...', or 'You do realise ..., don't you?' or 'I hope you're aware that...' to point out to someone else his or her obligation to   a) pay two weeks in advance   b) give a week's notice before leaving   c) pay for any damage to the furniture   d) wash the bath after using it   e) come back to the hotel before midnight every night   f) leave your passport with the manager.

Future arrangements

If you have already taken a step as part of a future plan, like buying a ticket for a train tomorrow, or booking a room for your holiday, you can then say things like

I'm leaving tomorrow
I'm/we're catching the early train
I'm spending my holidays in ... this year

In the same way, say you have arranged to   a) spend three months in England next year   b) go to a language school there   c) take a job later   d) go to Canada later.

Now talk about your real arrangements for   a) your next holiday   b) next weekend   c) this evening, after work or school.

Story telling/letter writing
You are John and have come back from holiday. Write a short account (150–200 words) of the first week in Bascome and the second week in the fishing village (Marston-on-Sea). Explain why you left Bascome earlier than planned and describe what happened between you and Miss Fox when you settled the bill.

This account may be in the form of a letter to a friend.

1·8a RIVALS

Look at the picture and discuss

Describe what is happening here.

What do you think the crowd is doing, and why?

How do you think the two girls, number 1 and 7, feel at the moment?

Pre-questions for the text

What are the two girls' names?

An earlier race is mentioned. What happened in it?

What is the name of the winner of this race? (In the picture.)

The huge outdoor athletics stadium was packed. Tension had been building up for the big event of the day, the Women's 1,500 metres. The two favourites, Alison Gould and Marcia Baker, were bitter rivals. As they warmed up in their track suits, they never once looked at each other.

    The two women resembled each other at least in appearance. They were both tall and slim. Alison's hair was blonde. Marcia's was a reddish colour. But whereas Alison was always grim and tight-lipped before a race, Marcia usually seemed relaxed, as if she did not really care. But this time things were different. As they went to their places at the starting line, Marcia looked even grimmer than Alison. The two had been in a race six weeks earlier. In the last few metres, just as Alison had seemed about to win, she had fallen. Marcia and another girl had been just behind her. Alison had lain on the track with cinders in her eyes and mouth and seen Marcia go on to win. Some people suspected, and Alison was among them, that Marcia had pushed her.

    Marcia waited tensely and nervously for the starter's gun. She was desperate to prove that she could win without any dirty tricks. In fact, she had been as surprised as everybody else when Alison had fallen, and had barely avoided doing so herself. She and the other eleven runners tensed. The gun cracked, and they were off.

    At first, the two rivals let others set the pace, and stayed in the middle of the tightly-bunched field. Then, with only two laps to go, Marcia moved up behind the two leaders. Alison went with her. They pounded into the final lap. Marcia went into the lead at the first bend. The crowd, sensing a close race, stood up and roared. Alison and two others gained ground on Marcia. Marcia began to sprint. Only she and Alison could stand that pace. They came round the last bend and into the straight neck and neck. Then, Alison inched ahead. Her lungs were bursting and her eyes were blurred, but she suddenly saw the tape and lunged. She felt it snap across her chest. She collapsed with the crowd's roars in her ears. Marcia stumbled past, her head hung in defeat.

1.8b

Text: comprehension and discussion

Multiple choice comprehension
Choose the *one* best answer: *a, b, c* or *d*.

1 Before the race began, Marcia was
a) careless *b)* relaxed *c)* tense
d) desperate.

2 Marcia went into the lead *a)* before the final lap *b)* at the very start
c) in the last few metres *d)* when Alison fell.

3 Just before the end of the race, Alison *a)* collapsed *b)* pushed Marcia
c) was pushed by Marcia *d)* went into the lead herself.

Vocabulary
Find the word or phrase that means
a) full of people *b)* nervous excitement *c)* people trying to beat each other *d)* looked like *e)* very serious, not happy *f)* small bits of coal or wood, partly burned *g)* not quite sure but ready to believe *h)* full circle around the track *i)* run fast
j) throw oneself forward *k)* fell down: could not stand any longer.

Comprehension and interpretation
Marcia particularly wanted to win this race. Explain why.

Do you think Marcia pushed Alison? Give reasons!

Describe both girls as best you can.

Put into words what Marcia was probably thinking to herself at the start.

How do you think she felt at the end? Why?

Question and answer (Interaction)
Work out questions and answers between someone who saw the race and someone who did not.

Possible question prompts
Very grim at the start?
Who – the pace at the beginning?
Marcia – into the lead?
Where – Alison at that point?
What – then? very close? etc.

Get a full description of the race!

Now explain *a)* They were *favourites*
b) the *field* was *tightly-bunched*
c) They *gained ground on* her. *d)* Her eyes were *blurred*.

Discussion and/or composition
'Suitable' and 'Unsuitable' sports for women. Consider the following. *Give reasons for your opinion* *a)* wrestling
b) gymnastics *c)* football
d) swimming *e)* weightlifting. Name and discuss others!

Related practice

You are a radio commentator. First orally and then in writing work out how you would describe the race from just before the start (warming up, taking off their track suits, going to their places, etc.) to just after the finish.

This commentary should be done using the forms

**is/are ... ing   is/are going to
has/have (done)**

Combine these forms with structures such as

**looks as if ...   is/has ...
... is definitely/probably going to ...**

Be sure to describe *a)* the stadium itself *b)* the final two laps. (The first half of the race can be left out. Simply say: 'And now we're in the third lap' and continue.)

Now do a short report (100–150 words) of a similar race between two men as the main rivals. This should be told as if you had seen the event some time in the past.

Begin *'When I got to the stadium, the runners were already warming up.'*
Use forms like
I could see that ...
was/were going to ...
They had just ... when ...
Suddenly ... Then, ...

32

1·8c

Listen to or read the dialogue
Alison's trainer, Jake Thomas, is congratulating her. The crowd is still roaring.

1

Jake: Wonderful! Great! Really beautiful!
Alison: (panting, out of breath) Thanks, Jake. Thanks. I... I... it was...
Jake: The best race you've ever run!
Alison: Oh, come on, Jake. Don't overdo it. But thanks all the same.
Jake: Just listen to that crowd! They all think it's great, too! *You're* great!
Alison: Oh, I... I don't really think I'm *that* good. But at least I won. It was a good race, wasn't it?
Jake: Yeah! Now... you'd better get into the dressing room. Get those things off!

2

And now Alison is in the dressing room. She is just about to leave, after showering and dressing.

Marcia: (tensely) Er... Alison!
Alison: (tense, too) Oh, hello, Marcia. I was...
Marcia: I just wanted to congratulate you! I mean, it was a good race and you deserved to win.
Alison: Well... thanks, Marcia. It's very nice of you to say so. I mean, ...
Marcia: It was that final sprint! You were great! Really!
Alison: Do you really think so? I mean, was I? Er... you... must be disappointed.

3

Marcia: I am! Very! I can't deny that! But I can't complain. There... there's something else I wanted to say. About the last race. When you fell.
Alison: Oh, don't think about that! Don't...
Marcia: No, let me finish, *please*. I know you must have at least suspected that I pushed you. But I didn't! Really!
Alison: Oh, I never really thought that!
Marcia: But it must have crossed your mind!
Alison: Well... to be frank... perhaps once or twice. But I never *really* thought so! *(fade)*

Exercises

Find the expressions here you could use when   a) you think someone whom you know well is giving you too much praise or does not really mean it   b) when you feel the praise is honest but do not want to appear 'big-headed'.

Answer with the correct tag and intonation as Alison does here.
Marcia: You were great! Really!
Alison: Do you really think so? I mean, was I?

And now Marcia says   a) You ran much better than I did   b) You could be a world champion!   c) You've got a lot of talent!   d) You're one of the best runners here!   e) You'll be in the next Olympic Games!

Modification

Rewrite sections 2 and 3 of the dialogue. It should be between two rivals in another sport, such as, for example, football, tennis, swimming or chess.

1·8d

Further practice

Open-ended dialogue
This dialogue occurred 6 weeks before the race described in *Rivals* and just after the race in which Alison fell. Marcia is talking to her trainer, Tony Duff. Fill in his part.

Tony: ___
Marcia: They suspect me of doing what to her? Pushing her! That's ridiculous.
Tony: ___
Marcia: Yes, but there were two other runners behind her as well!
Tony: ___
Marcia: Yes, of course we're rivals, but what does that prove! I just wouldn't do a thing like that!
Tony: ___
Marcia: But I don't hate her just because she's won a few races from me! And just who are these people who are saying such dreadful things about me?
Tony: ___
Marcia: But you must! You know what they're saying so you must know who they are!

Expressing suspicion

To suspect really means that you cannot be sure and have no proof, so you have to be careful about how you put it. Forms like

I can't help wondering if she pushed her
It almost looked to me as if she pushed her
It seemed to me that she might have pushed her

and even questions like

Do you think it's possible that she pushed her?

can all be used for this purpose. Use these different forms to show you suspect Marcia of a) kicking Alison b) putting poison in her tea c) hitting her in the back d) kicking cinders in her eye e) pulling her shirt in the last lap f) not really trying to win.

Reporting what they said

If you hear someone saying 'Marcia probably pushed her' and others agreeing, you can say later

Some people suspect Marcia of pushing Alison

Use this structure to report these things. Someone said (and others agreed)

She probably hates Alison
Perhaps she often plays dirty tricks like that
She is a poor sportswoman! Don't you think so?
I mean, it's possible she has done such things before
I can't help wondering if she doesn't win all her races unfairly!

Now say what you would suspect, and how you would express it, if a) people always fall ill after eating at a restaurant near the school b) a man without a job or rich parents always has big cars and a lot of money c) a factory that was not doing very well caught fire and the owner looked much happier and richer afterwards.

Congratulations

Probably the most common, if rather formal way of doing this is to say

I'd like to congratulate you on...ing

Use this form to congratulate someone just after they have a) got married b) passed the First Certificate Exam c) won the top prize in the 'Come Dancing' competition d) written the best composition in the class.

Letter writing
Your friend, John Neighbour, has just got married. His wife's name is Anna. Write a short note (100 words) congratulating him, hoping he has a good honeymoon, and ask him to keep in touch.
What do you think John would write back, a week later, in reply? (See 1.7a *Bad Way To Begin A Marriage*.)

34

1·9a Unlucky with Women

Look at the picture and discuss

What has just happened here?

What would you say if you were the man?

Has anything like this ever happened to you? Describe it.

Pre-questions for the text

Describe some of the 'unlucky' things that have happened to the man before.

Explain how the accident shown in the picture happened.

Denis had always been unlucky with women. Once, for example, he took one in his car for a drive. It broke down on a deserted country road and they had to walk for miles in the pouring rain to get to the nearest village. Another time he took a girl to a dance. But she had not told him about her jealous boyfriend, who punched Denis in the nose when he saw him with her there. Still another time, he went on a picnic with another girl. They were attacked by a swarm of bees. He was stung all over and so was she.

Denis had his eye on a girl named Mary, who worked in the same large office. He was trying to get up enough courage to invite her to a musical. One day he saw her standing in the self-service queue in the company canteen and managed to slip in just behind her. He decided to ask her then and there, but somehow he just could not think of the right words. She was wearing a new white dress and he complimented her on it.

As far as Mary was concerned, there were four types of men; those she could not stand, those she found dull and was indifferent to, those she was rather fond of, and last of all those she really liked. Denis was in the second category. He stuttered a few times and finally asked her to the musical. She politely but firmly turned him down. He tried again to persuade her but it was no use. They were still in the self-service queue.

Denis stared glumly at the thick, brown, steaming soup in a bowl on his tray. 'Oh, well. At least if I don't go out with her, nothing can go wrong,' he thought. When she went to a table, he followed her. She sat down and he was just about to do so himself when someone behind him called out his name. He swung around with the tray still in his hand. Suddenly he felt the hot, sticky soup dripping over his hand. The sudden motion had made the soup spill over. Then, with a sinking feeling in his stomach, he saw that the soup had also spilt on Mary's dress and that there were dark stains all over it. She was staring at them angrily.

1·9b

Text: comprehension and discussion

Multiple choice comprehension
Choose the *one* best answer: *a, b, c* or *d*.
1 Denis was the sort of man that Mary
a) was fond of   *b*) liked very much
c) felt nothing for   *d*) disliked.
2 When he asked her to the musical, she   *a*) got angry   *b*) refused   *c*) said nothing   *d*) laughed at him.

Vocabulary
Find the word or phrase that means
a) hit   *b*) line or row of people
c) boring, uninteresting   *d*) have difficulty in saying something   *e*) sadly, in a bad mood.

Comprehension and interpretation
Explain   *a*) who Mary and Denis were and where they worked   *b*) what he wanted to ask her in the queue   *c*) why she 'turned him down'   *d*) why Denis suddenly felt soup dripping over his hand   *e*) why he had a 'sinking feeling in his stomach' afterwards.

Describe   *a*) what Denis did when he saw her in the queue   *b*) what he probably said to her in the queue
c) what she probably said to him there
d) what happened then   *e*) what both of them probably said when he spilt the soup.

Question and answer (Interaction)
An hour ago, Denis told you he was going to ask Mary to a musical. He has come back from lunch. Ask him questions beginning

Well, did you . . . ?
And did she . . . ?
Why are you looking so . . . ?
Now get the whole story from him!

Now explain   *a*) The car *broke down*.
b) The road was *deserted*.   *c*) She had a *jealous* boyfriend.   *d*) He *swung around*.   *e*) There were *stains* all over the dress.

Discussion
Think of 'polite excuses' you can use when someone you do not like at all asks you to a party or film.

Related practice

**Once . . .   Another time . . .
Still another time . . .**

Write or tell a short story of about 80–100 words describing how unlucky you have been with your new car. Use phrases like

broke down   ran out of petrol
accident

You live in a flat. The man who lives above you is a very noisy neighbour. Complain to your landlord about him. Use phrases like

a wild party that went on till past midnight
an awful row with his girlfriend early in the morning
the television very loud one night

Describing likes and dislikes

**As far as I am concerned,
. . . cannot stand . . . ,
find dull/am indifferent to,
. . . rather fond of . . . ,
really like . . .**

Use these expressions *or others you think more suitable* to describe the way you feel about   *a*) food   *b*) films
c) television programmes.

In all three cases, describe the exact types of things you are talking about. about.

Invitations

**I'd like to invite you to . . .
I was wondering if you'd care to . . .
Would you like to . . . with me?**

Use one of the above to invite someone to   *a*) go on a picnic with you   *b*) have a drink in the pub round the corner this evening   *c*) play tennis   *d*) see a film.

1·9c

Listen to or read the dialogue
Denis has just slipped in behind Mary in the self-service queue.

1
Denis: Hello, Mary. How are you today?
Mary: (*not very enthusiastically*) Oh, hello Denis. All right, thanks. And you?
Denis: Oh, things could be worse. Er, ... new dress?
Mary: Sorry? What?
Denis: That dress you're wearing. Is it new?
Mary: Yes, it is. Why?
Denis: It's very nice. That's all.

2
Mary: Oh. You mean you like it?
Denis: Yes. I d ... do. (*pause*) Er, ... Mary. I was, I was ... w ... wond ... wondering if ... well, I was wondering if you'd care to see 'Skin'.
Mary: 'Skin'? What do you mean? Whose skin? What are you talking about?
Denis: It's a musical! Haven't you heard about it?
Mary: Oh! That 'Skin'. For a moment I thought you meant something else! (*pause*)

3
Denis: Well, what about it? As it happens, I've got two tickets for next Thursday evening. I thought perhaps ...
Mary: Well, thanks all the same, Denis. But ... no, I don't think so. Sorry.
Denis: It's supposed to be very good! I'm sure you'd enjoy it!
Mary: I'd like to, Denis, but I'm busy on Friday this week and next week, too.
Denis: But I said Thursday! The tickets are for Thursday evening!
Mary: Thursday? Oh, sorry. I meant Thursday, too. I mean, I'm busy then, too.
Denis: I see. Oh, well, some other time perhaps.
Mary: Yes, some other time perhaps. Thanks again.

Exercises
Give full explanations of exactly what is meant by the following phrases.

Example
Denis: New dress?

Explanation
Is that a new dress you're wearing? It's very nice.

Mary: All right, thanks. And you?
Mary: 'Skin'?
Denis: Well, what about it?
Mary: No, I don't think so.
Denis: Oh, well. Some other time, perhaps.
Mary: Yes, some other time, perhaps. Thanks all the same.

With books closed, take the role of Denis. Again, go through the dialogue part by part.

Do you think Mary is really busy on Thursday? Give reasons for your answer.

Modification
First orally and then in writing modify the dialogue based on these points.
a) Mary is very happy when Denis asks her how she is. She likes him.   *b)* He is wearing a new sports jacket. She compliments him on it.   *c)* She is giving a party for some friends next Saturday and invites him to it.   *d)* He has to visit his mother who is ill in hospital that evening. He is really sorry.   *e)* She suggests he should come after visiting his mother.   *f)* He says he will but that he may be late. He thanks her for inviting him.

Development
Denis has just spilt the soup on Mary. How do you think he apologises? Mary is very angry and is sure the spots will be difficult to get off.
What do you think she says?
How does Denis offer to pay for the cleaning bill?

1.9d

Further practice

Open-ended dialogue
Denis is talking to another girl, Jane.

Denis: ___
Jane: On Monday? Well, I'd like to and I like musicals, too. But I'm busy then.
Denis: ___
Jane: No, Tuesday evening would be all right.
Denis: ___
Jane: All right. At 7. In front of the theatre. Good idea! See you then.
Denis: ___
Jane: No, don't worry about that. I can easily get there by that time!

Turning down invitations

Study the following phrases

I'd really like to but I just can't. I'm so busy. I hope you understand

On...? Well, as it happens, I'm busy then. Is there any other time that would suit you?

No, I can't. Not then or any other time! Sorry!

Which of the three would Mary *most probably use* with someone she
a) cannot stand and does not care if she is rude to b) does not really like or dislike but does not want to be rude to c) likes very much but really cannot go out with at the time suggested.

Now turn down each of these invitations in at least *two* ways. The first time you are really busy but would like to find some other time. In the second case you do not want to be rude but have no interest in accepting the invitation at all.

I was wondering if you'd care to meet me for lunch on Monday.
There's a good film on this evening. Why don't we see it together?
Some friends and I are going to meet for coffee and a chat next Thursday. Would you like to come?

Accepting invitations and getting the time and place right

Denis is talking to another girl, Jane. Fill in her part, using phrases like 'Yes, I'd like to very much' and 'Yes, but where/when exactly do you want to ...?'

Denis: I was wondering if you'd like to see a film with me. A Western.
Jane: ___
Denis: Well, I was thinking about next Friday.
Jane: ___
Denis: It starts at 8.30. Can you be there by then?
Jane: ___
Denis: At the Classic cinema. That's in the centre of town near the bus station. Are you sure you can get there?
Jane: ___
Denis: Well, there's a number 22 bus that goes there. It stops on the corner across from where you live.

Composition dialogue writing
After this conversation, Denis broke his leg. This happened on Friday evening while he was trying to get to the bus stop himself. He fell while running for the bus and was taken to hospital.

First write out the conversation the next day when Denis phones Jane and explains why he did not come to the cinema.

Then write a short 'get-well' note from Jane to Denis. Begin

Dear Denis,
   I was terribly sorry to hear ...

and end with the phrase

   Yours sincerely

or any other you think suitable in the circumstances.

1·10a Two Strangers on a Train

Look at the picture and discuss

Where do you think the man and woman are?

He asked her something a moment ago. What do you think it was?

What do you think the woman is saying?

How do you feel about people smoking when you are eating?

Pre-questions for the text

The woman is unhappy about something in her own life. What?

Both people can help each other in a certain way. How?

Kate sat in the dining-car of the express train that was taking her back home to Bristol. She had hardly touched the meal in front of her. The steak was just as she normally liked it; medium-rare, thick and tender. It was surrounded by large, grilled mushrooms and crisp fried potatoes as well as boiled peas that for once were not overcooked. But Kate was worried and in a bad mood. She had recently come back to England from Mexico, where she had been very happy teaching English to businessmen and engineers. It seemed unlikely that she would ever find such a good job again. Two had been offered her, both of which she had turned down because of the poor salaries. Nobody seemed interested in her excellent qualifications, which included almost perfect Spanish, fluent German and French and an excellent knowledge of commercial and technical English.

Joe sat in another part of the train, smoking nervously. He was Director of Studies at a large English Language school in Cambridge which had recently started specialising in courses for foreign businessmen and engineers. He had a lot of problems. The one that bothered him most was finding good, qualified teachers who could teach the sort of English his students needed. A meeting of technical and commercial translators was taking place in Bristol, which was why he was going there. He hoped to persuade some of them to become teachers at his school, and was prepared to offer good salaries.

The only other person in Joe's compartment was an old man who was already asleep and snoring, and whose mouth was hanging open like an empty mouse-trap. Even though he was not hungry, he wondered if he might find more attractive company in the dining-car. The old man began to snore more loudly. Joe got up.

It was only after he had sat down in the one vacant seat in the dining-car that he noticed Kate. She was opposite him, and had the sort of face he liked. He wondered how he could start a conversation with her. He casually asked her if she minded him smoking, feeling sure she would not. But to his surprise, she did. She pointed to a no smoking sign, which he had not noticed. Nothing more was said for a moment. Then, as he looked at her, Joe suddenly felt sure he had met her somewhere before.

Text: comprehension and discussion

Multiple choice comprehension
Choose the *one* best answer: *a, b, c* or *d*.
1 Kate was going to Bristol because she *a*) lived there *b*) worked there *c*) wanted a job there *d*) had to attend a meeting.
2 Joe sat down opposite Kate because he *a*) thought he knew her *b*) liked her face *c*) wanted to talk to her *d*) could not find another seat.

Vocabulary
Find the word or phrase that means
a) can be easily cut and chewed
b) cooked directly on or under the fire
c) cooked so that it is still firm, cracks when you chew it *d*) breathe noisily when asleep.

Now explain *a*) She *hardly touched* the meal. *b*) It seemed *unlikely*. *c*) She had *turned* the jobs *down*. *d*) He was *prepared* to offer good *salaries*. *e*) She had good *qualifications*.

Comprehension and interpretation
Describe *a*) Kate's meal *b*) her job in Mexico *c*) her qualifications *d*) Joe's job *e*) the passenger in his compartment *f*) what happened in the dining-car.

Explain *a*) why Kate was worried *b*) why Joe was going to Bristol *c*) why he was surprised when he asked Kate if he could smoke.

Interaction
Interview Kate for a job. Find out about her *a*) qualifications *b*) previous job *c*) knowledge of foreign languages.
What else would you want to know?

Joe offers you a job at his school. What questions would you ask about *a*) salary *b*) hours *c*) other things?

Related practice

who/that   whose   which/that   where

Use these in the sentences below. Note that in *some* but not *all* cases, 'that' can be substituted for 'who' or 'which'.

Kate was going to Bristol, *(a)* her parents lived. She was thinking about the two jobs *(b)* had been offered her, neither of *(c)* she had taken. Meanwhile Joe was staring at the old man *(d)* was sitting opposite him and *(e)* snoring was beginning to disturb him. He decided to go to the dining-car. *(f)* he hoped to find a more attractive travelling companion. He sat down at a small table, opposite a girl *(g)* face he did not at first recognise. He was smoking a cigarette. *(h)* was forbidden there. The girl pointed to a sign *(i)* he had not noticed before and *(j)* said 'No Smoking'.

Describing food

Study the way Kate's food is described in the first paragraph. Then compare it with the description of the hotel food in the second paragraph of *A Bad Way To Begin A Marriage* (1.7). What are the differences?

Now first orally and then in writing describe *two* meals, one of which you enjoyed and the other of which you did not. Give reasons.

Now describe how you like things like meat and vegetables cooked, using terms like
rare/medium-rare/well-done
crisp/tender/heavily or delicately flavoured with garlic, pepper, etc.

1·10c

Listen to or read the dialogue
Kate is in the dining-car. Joe has just come in.

1

Joe: Excuse me. Is anyone sitting here?
Kate: No. Nobody. *(He sits down. Pause)*
Joe: You don't mind if I smoke, do you?
Kate: Well, . . . to be frank, yes, I *do*!
Joe: (surprised) Oh, I'm sorry. *(doubtful, uncertain)* But this isn't a no-smoker, is it? I mean, after all, . . .
Kate: Actually, it *is*! Perhaps you haven't noticed the sign.
Joe: Sign? What sign?
Kate: There! On the window!
Joe: Oh, sorry. I didn't realise. Sorry!
Kate: Don't mention it.
(Joe puts out his cigarette. Pause)

2

Joe: Excuse me, but haven't we met somewhere before? Recently, I mean.
Kate: (rather icily) I don't think so. I mean, I doubt it somehow.
Joe: Oh? Why?
Kate: I was out of the country for a long time until very recently.
Joe: I'm sure we *have*, you know. Where?
Kate: Where? I'm afraid I don't understand.
Joe: Which country were you in? Wait a moment! Let me remember. It . . . um . . . might have been Venezuela or . . . er . . . I've got it! It must have been Mexico! Yes! Weren't you in Mexico City?

3

Kate: (surprised) Yes, that's right. How . . . how did you know?
Joe: Because I was there on business last winter. Weren't you teaching there?
Kate: Yes. English to businessmen and engineers. But how . . . ?
Joe: We met at a party there!
Kate: Are you sure we *did*? I mean, I'm sorry, but I can't remember ever meeting you before.
Joe: Yes, I *am*! In fact, I'm positive!

Exercises

Find these phrases in the text. Then explain their full meaning.
Example
Kate: Actually, it *is*.
Explanation
Actually, it is a no-smoker.

Kate: To be frank, yes, I *do*.
Kate: I don't think so. I mean, I doubt it somehow.
Joe: I'm sure we *have*, you know.
Kate: Are you sure we *did*?

Now explain to someone else   a) why Kate at first does not think she and Joe have met before   b) how Joe knows so much about her.

Go through the dialogue part by part. Take the role of *either* Kate or Joe.

Open-ended dialogue
What do you think Kate is saying?
Kate: ___
Joe: I think it was on New Year's Eve.
Kate: ___
Joe: That's right! A Scotsman gave it.
Kate: ___
Joe: Yes! Exactly! MacKay was his name.
Kate: ___
Joe: Well, there were a lot of people there. Perhaps that's why. And I've got a very ordinary face.

Development
Finish the dialogue, based on these points

Kate asks about Joe's job. He tells her.

Joe asks what she is doing now. He is surprised to hear she has not found a good job yet.

Kate asks for advice about how to find one. He suggests she should come to Cambridge for an interview. She accepts.

They arrange an interview in two weeks' time.

Further practice

Expressing doubt

Here are some common ways of doing this

**I don't think that we've met before
I rather doubt that you really know me
It's rather unlikely that we met in Mexico**

Talk about yourself. Express doubt that you *a)* will live until the age of 120 *b)* can learn languages in your sleep *c)* speak perfect English *d)* will become the richest person in the world *e)* could learn 5 languages perfectly.

What are some other things you doubt?

But also notice that when Joe doubts that

This is a no-smoker

he says

This isn't a no-smoker, is it?

Note the intonation on the tape. Doubt all the things above in the same way!

Showing you are almost certain

Questions
When Joe asks Kate if they have met before, he is almost certain they have. So he asks

Excuse me, but haven't we met before?

You are talking to Kate. Make these sentences into the same type of question.

Your name is Kate Martin
You taught English in Mexico City
You were there last year
You came to Don MacKay's party!
You speak four languages
I've seen you somewhere before

Asking for permission

When Joe asks Kate if he can smoke, he is almost sure she will not mind. So he says

You don't mind if I smoke, do you?

In the same way, ask someone else for permission (you are almost sure you will get it) to *a)* open the window *b)* close the door *c)* turn up the radio *d)* use the phone *e)* borrow some paper *f)* go home early.

Look at these three ways of reporting what was said.

He **was sure** that he **had met** her before. (Certainty)
She **thought** that they **might have met** in Mexico. (Possible, not certain)
She **doubted** that he **had met** her before. (Very unlikely)

Now report each of Kate's statements in one of the three ways.

Joe: Let's see. Perhaps I met you in Venezuela.
Kate: I don't think so somehow.
Joe: But I must have met you somewhere before!
Kate: Hmm. Perhaps you saw me in Mexico City.
Joe: Yes! I remember now! I saw you teaching. Definitely!
Kate: Well, perhaps you did.
Joe: Or . . . wait a moment . . . perhaps I saw you at MacKay's party.
Kate: Oh, come now. You didn't really come to it, did you?
Joe: Yes, really! I remember now! We had a long talk! Yes!

Composition
You want to work in an English-speaking country. An agency called 'International Jobs' (which offers a wide range of work) may be able to find something for you. Describe to them your *a)* education *b)* age *c)* knowledge of languages *d)* main interests and hobbies. (120–150 words)

Write about what you think is likely to happen and what you doubt will happen within the next 60 years. Among other things, give your opinion about such things as *a)* wars breaking out *b)* new forms of transport *c)* men going to other planets *d)* women becoming completely equal with men.

Section Two *Interviews*

This is Michele Parks

She interviews famous people. She has a famous 'talk' programme on radio and TV.

Some people hate talk programmes, and her talk programme in particular. But a lot of other people like such programmes.

How do you feel about talk programmes? Do you ever listen to them? Why? Or why not?

In this section, Michele Parks interviews

1 Another interviewer who has interviewed some of the most powerful and famous people of our time

2 Two people who argue about whether 'to smoke or not to smoke'

3 A very popular entertainer sometimes called 'The King of Bad Taste'

4 A politician and a sports writer who argue about 'football hooliganism'

5 An expert on sharks and another man who was almost eaten by one

What this section contains	This section has five Units of Material. Each Unit consists of one interview (first two pages); two pages of exercise based on the interview (last two pages of each Unit); the interviews themselves are always recorded.
This section deals with the skills of	Use of English (Paper 3); Composition (Paper 1); Listening comprehension (Paper 4).
Some of the things you will learn in this section	Among other things in this section, you will learn ways of insisting on things agreeing and disagreeing showing that you either approve or do not approve of things giving opinions and making proposals getting other people's opinions correcting people expressing opinions which you think may be wrong.

Suggestions to the teacher

Using recordings in the presentation
As with the other two sections in the book, the use of taped or cassette material is *optional*. However, where it is possible or suitable to use it, there are at least two alternative procedures.

Play each part of the interview *twice*. Ask no questions after the first time. The second time, keep stopping the tape each time you come to a question. (Those printed on the left-hand side can, and of course usually should, be supplemented by those you think necessary for your particular class.)

Play each part of the interview completely, without stopping. Then, see if the class can answer a complete range of questions all at once. If they cannot answer a particular question, do *not* supply the answer. Keep the question in mind and see if it can be answered after a second playing. Both procedures can be used at different times with the same class.

If you do not use the recorded materials the interview can be presented in the same way you would any other printed text.

The questions
It is strongly recommended that those printed next to the interview itself should always be done before the multiple choice comprehension. If the presentation is with books closed, ask the questions as you go along.

The multiple choice items in this section as in the other two sections, are here mainly in order to accustom students to this form of question, *not* because such questions are the best way to teach. These multiple-choice items should always be done only after all three parts of the interview have been done.

Homework and other exercises
All exercises in parts *b* and *c* of each Unit can be used for homework. All those in *Further practice* should always be done orally first. The summary (bottom right-hand fourth page) is particularly important as preparation for the examination, and should be done in writing at home even if first done orally in class.

Compositions can often be discussed in class first.

Language notes on the interviews

Accents: McDine (1) and Stapatski (3) both have American accents on the recordings. Marston (4) speaks with a slight trace of a Northern English accent. Laster (5) speaks with an Australian accent. Standard colloquial 'spoken' grammar is used throughout

2·1a The Powerful and the Famous

 Michele Parks interviews another interviewer, Walter J. McDine. McDine is famous in the United States and Britain for his 'hard-hitting, searching, often brutal' interviews, particularly of well-known politicians.

1

Parks: Walter J. McDine, you have interviewed some of the most powerful and famous people in our time. Why do you think television interviews are better than those on radio?

Do you agree? Why?

McDine: Because it's important not only to hear but also to see the person I'm interviewing.

Parks: But why? I should have thought it was enough simply to hear what is being said. After all, ...

What does 'selling favours' mean? And what is said here which helps to explain it?

McDine: Not if you think about it. For example, suppose I'm interviewing a politician who's been accused of selling favours ...

Parks: In other words, using his position and influence to help other people earn money.

Would you suppose the politician was lying if he did this? Explain why ... or why not.

McDine: Exactly. Now when he denies these accusations, his voice is quite firm. But perhaps his mouth twitches or a look of fear comes into his eyes ... or he doesn't look me ... the interviewer ... straight in the eye. If you can see these things as well as hear him, you can perhaps judge a little better whether or not he's actually telling the truth. Or to put it another way, TV's more revealing.

2

Explain the meaning of 'vain'. Then use it in one or two examples of your own.

Parks: Is it true, by the way, that politicians are just as vain as film stars? Do they really worry so much about how they look?

McDine: Well, vanity's something almost everybody suffers from, particularly on TV where you can be seen by millions of people. I think I would say that in this respect politicians can be ... how ... how shall I put it ... very ... uh ... skilful.

Suppose you are a political leader and are being interviewed on TV. Would *you* be worried about how you look? Why?

Parks: Skilful? How do you mean?

McDine: Let me give you an example. Not long ago there was an American President ... I won't tell you which one ... who'd been a football player in his

45

youth. And his nose had been broken. Now you could see this particularly if you looked at him from the left.

Parks: In other words, his left profile wasn't the same as his right profile.

McDine: No, it wasn't. His right profile in fact seemed quite normal. You couldn't see his nose had been broken from that side at all. Now ... in his speeches on TV, he always made sure that the cameras got him from his *left* side when he wanted to seem a man of action ... hard ... the man who could get things done ... and in those parts of his speech when he wanted to seem pleasant and nice ... the man who could bring other people together ... he made sure that the cameras got him from the *right*. In other words, he used the two different sides of his face to great effect at different times.

> Explain how this American President used the two sides of his face in his TV speeches.
>
> Then explain *why* you think he showed his broken nose when he wanted to appear a 'man of action'.

3

Parks: In your own interviews you always use three cameras, don't you? Why is that?

McDine: Mainly in order to keep the viewer's attention and to focus on different things at different times. Interviews are more effective that way.

Parks: What's the function of each camera?

McDine: Well, the first camera is stationary. It's kept on the same thing all the time. That is, it's kept on the person I'm interviewing.

Parks: And the second camera?

McDine: That's the action camera. It moves about ... it focuses on small details. For example, it might give a close-up of the politician's mouth ... so that we can see it um ... twitching when certain questions are asked.

Parks: You mean, you can show if he's lying?

McDine: If you want to put it that way, yes.

Parks: What about the third camera?

McDine: It's usually kept either on me or on the audience. In that way, the director can cut back and forth from camera to camera during the interview.

Parks: Walter J. McDine. Thank you.

> Explain what the second camera does.
> Then describe how *you* would feel if you knew that while you were being interviewed on TV, a camera was doing this.
>
> Explain in what way you think these three cameras help to keep the viewer's attention

2·1b

Text: comprehension and discussion

Multiple choice comprehension
Find the *one* best answer: *a, b, c* or *d*.

1. McDine says TV interviews are better than radio interviews because *a)* they are always more interesting *b)* it is easier to judge whether someone is lying or not *c)* it is easier to lie on radio *d)* people do not try to lie as much.

2. When a person twitches, he or she *a)* makes a sudden, nervous movement *b)* makes an impolite noise *c)* begins to argue *d)* shows that he or she does not like something.

3. McDine says he has found politicians to be very skilful on TV in *a)* hiding their vanity *b)* telling lies *c)* using it to give the right impression of themselves to the viewers *d)* always appearing pleasant and nice.

4. To do something with *great effect* means you *a)* go to a great deal of trouble *b)* spend a great deal of time and money *c)* make a very big mistake *d)* do it very successfully.

5. The three cameras in McDine's programmes *a)* are not really necessary *b)* each have different functions *c)* do different things at different times *d)* cut back and forth all the time.

6. A stationary camera is one that *a)* moves only now and then *b)* moves all the time *c)* moves only with other cameras *d)* never moves at all.

Discussion
A boy in school is accused of stealing. He twitches and goes very red in the face. What are some possible reasons for this?

Related practice

Reformulation
That is, . . .   In other words, . . .
Or to put it another way, . . .

These are often used before you say the *same thing again in a different way*. Use them now.

Politicians are vain. They worry too much about their appearance.

He has a sugar side. He looks better from the right than from the left.

He's tough. He's ready to fight and difficult to beat!

And now use them again while explaining what is meant by

The camera must be kept stationary.

We want a head and shoulders shot.

People often lie with their mouths but tell the truth with their faces.

Describing people's reactions
His mouth twitched.
She went pale and as white as a sheet.
He looked him straight in the eye.
Her eyes were red and her face was wet with tears.
He went very red in the face.
Her eyes were blazing with anger.
A look of fear came into his eyes.

These are only a few of the ways you might describe people's reactions. Which of these would you use to describe *a)* a man whose new car has just been scratched *b)* a very angry woman *c)* a woman who has just received terrible news *d)* a man who is not afraid of another one *e)* someone under great nervous pressure *f)* someone who has been crying *g)* a small man facing a very large and angry dog in a dark street.

Describe other things like *a)* a liar *b)* a man who suddenly finds he is not wearing any trousers *c)* a child caught stealing, etc.

2.1c

Further practice

Insisting on things

There are many ways you can insist. For example

**I've simply got to . . .
Unless you . . . , I won't . . .
It's absolutely essential that you should . . .
I'll . . . only on condition that you . . .**

You are going to be interviewed. Use one of these forms to insist that *a)* you get paid at least £500 *b)* you are seen only from your sugar side *c)* you are asked only 'impersonal' questions *d)* you get plenty of time to study them first *e)* you are interviewed only by the 'star interviewer'.

Now think of other things you would insist on and how you would do it *a)* in a restaurant where you are taking people in order to impress them *b)* at a private language school you are sending your young daughter to *c)* with someone you are going to pay to decorate your house or flat.

Reporting it

If a film star says: 'I must be seen only from my sugar side!', you can later say

He insisted on being seen only from his sugar side

In the same way, report these other things he said. You overheard them.

Unless I can have my girl friend with me, there'll be no interview!
I'm going to wear special make-up!
I'll do this only on condition that I can direct the interview myself!
I must appear only in special light!
I've simply got to drink champagne during the interview!

Word formation

Use the word on the left in another form.

Example
appear Some people are too interested in their **appearance**.

accuse Many ___ were made.
vain What terrible ___ !
deny Nobody believed his ___ .
skill The way he used TV was very ___ .
effect The technique was very ___ .
prove The fact that his mouth twitched is not ___ that he was lying.

Interaction

You did not see the Michele Parks interview with McDine. A friend did. Find out from the friend *a)* about McDine himself (Who? Why . . . famous? What kind of people . . . ?) *b)* what your friend found most interesting in the interview.

Summary

Summarise what McDine said. The summary should concentrate on answers to these questions.

In what way does he think TV is better for interviews than radio?

How does it help to see the person being interviewed?

Give an example of how politicians can be skilful in using TV.

Explain how and why McDine uses three cameras in his interviews.

Composition

Write between 120 and 180 words on one of these topics.

Briefly describe the advantages and disadvantages of watching an important sporting event (for example, an international football match) on TV or going to the stadium itself. *or*

What are the TV or radio programmes you most enjoy watching or listening to?

48

2·2a   To Smoke or Not to Smoke?

 Michele Parks interviews two people with very different opinions. One is Julia Halewood, an advertising executive. She is also the leader of the 'Campaign Against Smoking in Public Places', or CASP for short. The other is Daniel Paul, a novelist and film writer.

1

Parks: Smoking used to be considered fashionable. But now people like you, Julia Halewood, are suggesting that it's anti-social, even almost criminal. Could you tell us why?

Julia: Look at the facts. As a nation we spend more on tobacco than we do on educating our children or on doctors, medicine and hospitals. Smokers, of course, are far more likely to come down with diseases like cancer or chronic bronchitis, and have to be treated at the nation's expense. But not only do they ruin their own health but that of others as well. They force us to inhale the poison they blow into the air. This, of course, is dreadfully anti-social behaviour.

Parks: Well, what do you suggest ought to be done?

Julia: First, double the tax on all forms of tobacco. Second, ban all forms of tobacco advertising. Third, ban smoking itself in all restaurants, trains, public meeting-places and places like schools and hospitals. And fourth, protect young people more than we do now.

Parks: What kind of protection did you have in mind?

Julia: Among other things we could double or triple the fines on anyone who sells tobacco to people under the age of 18. And we could and must intensify our efforts to educate young people – to show them the dreadful effects of this dreadful habit!

2

Parks: Daniel Paul. What's your reaction to this?

Paul: It seems an exaggeration, to say the least. I don't deny that smoking can be harmful. But so can lots of other habits. Eating sweets, for example.

Julia: Oh, I just can't accept that there's any comparison between the two habits! And I very much doubt that anybody else can, either.

What do you think she means by 'anti-social'?

In what way does smoking appear an expensive habit, according to Julia Halewood?

Describe the four things she would like to do.

How can young people be protected?

What do *you* think of the comparison?

2·2a

In what way is sugar bad, according to Daniel Paul?

Paul: Perhaps you'd let me finish. Lots of people die because they eat far too much sugar. Not only does it cause things like tooth-decay, it makes people overweight, as well. And as a result they often die of heart-attacks. But there's no tax on sweets, and no campaign to ban them, either.

Julia: Of course too much sugar is bad. But who's harmed by it? Only the person who eats too much!

Paul: Just a moment. On the one hand you want to ban smoking in restaurants because you say the smoke is bad for non-smokers. But on the other hand you say nothing about motor cars. You don't really believe that smoking causes as much pollution as motor cars, do you?

In what way do motor cars cause pollution?

Julia: Of course I don't. But . . .

Paul: Then why don't you try to ban cars from public places, as well? From the roads, for instance.

3

Julia: Motor cars at least serve some useful purpose.

Paul: You can hardly expect smokers to give up the simple pleasure of a cigar or cigarette after a good meal in a restaurant.

How do *you* feel about people smoking when you are in a restaurant?

Julia: Quite the contrary! You can hardly expect non-smokers to have the simple pleasure of actually tasting the food ruined by selfish and thoughtless smokers!

Paul: Aren't you going a bit too far when you say that we actually *ruin* the pleasure of tasting the food? You don't really believe that, do you?

Parks: Well, we'll come back to that question after a short break for a song. And its title, strangely enough, is 'Smoke keeps getting in my eyes'. And here to sing it is Edith Montgomery.

2.2b

Text: comprehension and discussion

Multiple choice comprehension
Choose the *one* best answer: *a, b, c* or *d*.

1 The main reason Julia Halewood thinks smoking is anti-social seems to be because   *a)* it is so expensive   *b)* smokers harm themselves   *c)* people do not object enough to it   *d)* smokers harm themselves and others.

2 She wants to *ban* tobacco-advertising, or   *a)* allow it only at certain times   *b)* not allow it at all   *c)* put a tax on it   *d)* attack those who do it.

3 Smokers *come down* with cancer, or   *a)* die of it   *b)* cause others to die of it   *c)* suffer from the disease   *d)* do not realise they will get it.

4 Daniel Paul believes that Julia   *a)* makes smoking sound worse than it is   *b)* is more or less correct in what she says   *c)* is herself overweight because she eats too much sugar   *d)* should not compare smoking and eating sweets.

5 *Pollution* is   *a)* something caused only by cars   *b)* a type of disease smokers get   *c)* dirt, bad air and things like that   *d)* any bad habit which causes a disturbance.

6 How does Daniel Paul feel about smoking in restaurants?   *a)* he sees nothing really wrong in it   *b)* he agrees it is a very unpleasant thing   *c)* he says smokers must expect to give it up   *d)* he says he never does it himself.

Discussion
Which ideas or facts in particular do you think ought to be communicated in an advertising campaign *against* smoking?
Now try to think of arguments or ideas *in favour* of a smoker's right to smoke.

Related practice

Contrasts and comparisons

On the one hand...   On the other...
Quite the contrary!

Which sentences below would you use these with? And how?

You say smoking isn't really dangerous. You say children should not do it.

I don't advertise tobacco. I refuse to have anything to do with it.

She attacks smoking as a nasty habit. She smokes herself.

I don't mind people smoking cigars. I actually like the smell.

I didn't enjoy the film. I fell asleep in the middle of it.

He believes smoking is dangerous. He smokes like a chimney himself.

I don't dislike the smell of a good cigar. I can't stand cigarette smoke.

Describing habits
particularly other people's

...ing is a	nasty revolting pleasant inoffensive	habit
I can't stand I detest I don't mind I see nothing wrong with		people who...

Use these, or other ways you can think of, to describe your attitude to such things as   *a)* smoking pipes, cigars or cigarettes   *b)* chewing tobacco and spitting it out   *c)* laughing and singing loudly in public   *d)* playing transistor radios in public   *e)* letting dogs run wild or foul the pavement   *f)* arguing, losing one's temper, swearing.

Now think of some other habits like this that you find either very bad or have nothing against!

Further practice

Disagreeing

I don't altogether agree that smoking is so bad
I just can't accept that smoking is so bad
I very much doubt that it isn't harmful
I reject the idea that it isn't harmful
It's completely wrong to say it isn't harmful

These are only a few of the ways of disagreeing. Use them now (one or more) to disagree with the following statements.

Smoking doesn't cause any diseases.
There's nothing wrong with children doing it.
Smoking is very fashionable and chic.
Smoking is good for the nerves.
It doesn't really harm people.

You can also *suggest* disagreement by asking questions like

How can you really say that smoking …?
You don't really believe … do you?
Aren't you going a bit too far when you say …?

Disagree in this way with statements like

Smoking is worse than war!
It is a criminal act!
All smokers are anti-social!
Tobacco was invented by the devil!
One cigarette can kill you!

Agreeing

I agree that smoking can be harmful
I accept that smoking can be harmful
I also think that it causes many diseases
I entirely agree that it causes many diseases

First of all go through the interview again. Then agree with any of the things that either Julie Halewood or Daniel Paul says.

Then look through it a second time. Are there any statements you would strongly disagree with? If so, what are they and how would you do it?

Word formation

Find the correct form of the word on the left so that it can be used on the right.

expensive These diseases are treated at the nation's ___.
behave Is smoking really anti-social ___?
exaggerate Her speech is full of ___.
protect Non-smokers need more ___.
harm Is smoking really so ___?

Interaction

A friend is walking about with a CASP button on his or her shirt (see introduction to this interview). Your friend, like Julia Halewood, is very sensitive about people smoking in restaurants, etc.

Find out *a)* exactly what CASP means *b)* why he or she is a member *c)* about the diseases he or she thinks are caused by smoking *d)* what he or she wants the Government or other people to do.

Then either agree or disagree with your friend's suggestions.

Summary

Use these questions as guides in summarising the points made by Julia Halewood and Daniel Paul.

In what way is smoking harmful for smokers?
In what way do smokers cause problems for non-smokers?
What does Julia Halewood suggest doing in order to stop people smoking?
Why is Daniel Paul against these things?

Composition

Write between 150 and 200 words about one of these topics.

A short letter giving advice to a friend who smokes 40 cigarettes a day. Suggest how he can give it up. *or*
Arguments in favour of a smoker's right to smoke.

2·3a The King of Bad Taste

 Michele Parks interviews a very rich and famous popular entertainer; a pianist who plays classical music in a wildly romantic and spectacular way. He is also famous for his extravagant clothes and three huge pianos, which, as he will tell you, do some very unusual things. His name is 'Stapatski'.

1

Explain what you think he means by 'I cry all the way to the bank'.

Parks: Stapatski. You have been called 'The King of Bad Taste'. Does that disturb you?
Stapatski: Oh, yeah. I cry all the way to the bank.
Parks: You mean it's all right as long as you make money?
Stapatski: Well, once a critic said I ought to be horsewhipped for playing music the way I do. But all I really do is give people what they want. What's so terrible about that. Besides, who can really decide what good taste is and what is bad? Can you tell me that? What's 'bad taste'?

Listen to Parks' voice carefully. Do you really think she agrees?

Parks: Hmm. Perhaps you have a point . . . but let me turn to your career now. I mean, when you began as a pianist, you . . . how shall I put it . . . you stuck to the usual conventions, didn't you?

Describe how Stapatski dressed at the beginning of his career.

Stapatski: If you mean, did I wear one of those black suits and ties that made me look like a head-waiter, and look solemn and miserable when I played . . . as if I were at a funeral . . . the answer is 'Yes'. But not for long. I soon developed my own style.

2

Parks: Just where . . . and how did you begin to develop your 'own style' . . . as you call it?

What do you think he means by 'the big time'?

Stapatski: Well, as you know I was born and raised in New York City . . . in America . . . and after I left the conservatory of music where I studied, I started giving piano recitals in small towns . . . you know, all over America. I wasn't in the big time in those days. Well, anyway . . . one evening I was in . . . oh, I can't remember exactly, but I think it was in Wisconsin . . . and if I'm not mistaken the audience consisted mostly of rich farmers. And they were all sitting there like a lot of sleeping zombies . . . if you know what I mean . . . it was a really hot

Describe the audience, the weather and Stapatski that evening.

evening and there I was practically glued to my piano stool in my own sweat. It was dripping off me. And . . . let me see, as far as I can remember I was playing

2·3a

something by Chopin . . . and I could see . . . well . . . feel, I mean . . . that they just weren't enjoying it and were ready to fall off their chairs with boredom. So I stopped playing and stood up.

Parks: You mean, you stopped in the middle of a piece?

Stapatski: Exactly. And I shouted something like . . . oh . . . I can't remember exactly . . . 'Come on, now, folks. What would you really like to hear?' Well, at first they looked at me as if I were a madman, but at least they were all awake. Someone tittered, but someone else called out 'What about "Old MacDonald had a farm"?' That's a . . . a . . .

Parks: Nursery song. Very simple. Yes.

Stapatski: Yeah. Kids sing it. Well, since they were bored with Chopin and so was I, and since they wanted me to do something else . . . I just did it. But I didn't just play it as a simple song. Instead I played it in a kind of wild Chopin style . . . really wild, if you know what I mean . . . and they loved it . . . lapped it up . . . went wild . . .

Why were they suddenly all awake?

What exactly did he do?

3

Parks: And soon after that you started playing night clubs.

Stapatski: Yes. Because I decided first of all to play Bach and Beethoven and Chopin in a very popular style . . . romantic, too . . . and also to give people a real . . . spectacle. I started wearing fancy clothes . . . a suit of mine lights up in the dark when I play and glows like a Christmas tree . . . I've got another suit that's made of silver and diamonds . . .

Parks: And your three pianos. They . . .

Stapatski: They're a special part of my act. I've got to have three because I do three different kinds of shows. One piano is for the shows I do for younger people . . . it's black . . . like a coffin . . . but it lights up, too . . . and makes other noises as well . . . it's got a motorcycle horn and other things on it . . . a special device, for example that sounds like a big drum. And then the second piano is for night clubs. It's a bit smaller, and it's all white with diamonds in it . . . diamonds that sparkle and glow . . . and the third piano is the one I play at home. It's got a big mirror and a spotlight on it . . . and play it only for friends.

Parks: I gather your father . . . who still lives in New York . . . doesn't approve of all this.

Stapatski: Right. Dad's a bit odd. He . . . he paid for my music lessons when I was a kid . . . and really loves the old composers. And he often says 'How can you do such a thing, son? It's terrible of you to play Bach and Chopin that way.' Even when I show him all the money I earn now, he still doesn't approve. Old people are a bit strange, I guess.

Describe what you would expect to hear and see if you went to one of Stapatski's shows for younger people.

Describe the differences between his night club acts and his shows for younger people.

Why doesn't his father approve?

2.3b

Text: comprehension and discussion

Multiple choice comprehension
Choose the *one* best answer: *a, b, c* or *d*.

1 When asked about bad taste, Stapatski *a)* agrees he is guilty of it   *b)* admits he is worried about it   *c)* says it is not really easy to define what 'bad taste' is   *d)* claims that people want only bad taste.

2 Stapatski *stuck to the usual conventions*. *a)* He did what other pianists did. *b)* He found them hot and uncomfortable. *c)* He decided to break them. *d)* He studied them carefully.

3 At the beginning of his recital that night in Wisconsin, the audience *a)* was too stupid to understand the music *b)* was very bored with it *c)* applauded wildly when he played Chopin *d)* listened politely and with some interest.

4 Someone *tittered* in the audience. That is, *a)* someone laughed loudly   *b)* this person got very angry   *c)* Stapatski could hear a kind of whisper   *d)* someone laughed but not loudly.

5 The audience *lapped it up*. They *a)* did not understand it   *b)* laughed with embarrassment   *c)* clearly liked it very much   *d)* almost laughed him off the stage.

6 Stapatski is surprised that his father *a)* still likes the old composers *b)* disapproves at all of what he is doing   *c)* disapproves despite all the money earned   *d)* thinks it is odd so much can be earned.

Discussion

Give some examples of what you consider 'bad' and 'good taste' in *a)* the way other people dress *b)* furniture and home decoration *c)* behaviour at events like funerals, concerts and formal parties.

Related practice

Not being 100 per cent certain about what you remember

If I'm not mistaken . . .
As far as I can remember . . .
If I remember correctly . . .
I can't remember exactly but I think . . .

Use one of these to show you are not 100 per cent certain that *a)* you saw Stapatski a few years ago   *b)* he was wearing a suit of diamonds and silver   *c)* there were 20,000 in the audience   *d)* the concert lasted $2\frac{1}{2}$ hours   *e)* he played a song called 'Old MacDonald'.

Give answers to these questions, too. Show you are not completely certain.

When did you get up last Sunday?
How many people were there in your very first English class?
How much did you pay for a meal the last time you ate in a restaurant?

Now think of more questions you can ask which would get such answers. Give the answers as well.

Describing an audience's reactions

Study Stapatski's own description of his audience when he played the first piece of Chopin and then 'Old MacDonald'. ('They sat there like . . . You could have cut the silence with a knife. They went wild.' etc.)

Describe what you would expect an audience to do that *a)* is very bored by a performance   *b)* is reasonably interested but not wild   *c)* likes something very much but is rather 'formal'   *d)* really dislikes a performance.

Use such verbs as
to hiss/to boo loudly/to applaud enthusiastically/to sit there in deep silence/to fall asleep.

Further practice

Disapproval

Here are just a few ways of expressing this

**I think it's terrible of you to . . .
I really think you shouldn't . . . !
I really disapprove of you . . . ing!**

You have a brother who does the following things. Tell him you disapprove.

He spends all his money on drink.
He beats his children.
He treats his wife like a slave.
He borrows money and does not pay it back.
He tells all sorts of lies.

Imagine that an old man is talking about all the things young people do today which he disapproves of. What are some of the things he would say to his own grandchildren who do these things?

Approving/not disapproving

**I don't see anything wrong in . . . ing
What's so terrible about . . . ing?
I think it's a good thing that . . .**

Use one of these to show either that you approve or at least do not disapprove of things like   *a*) playing Bach the way Stapatski does
b) playing classical music in 'popular versions'   *c*) giving people what they want   *d*) making serious music into a spectacle   *e*) earning money this way.

Now look back over 'To Smoke or not to Smoke' again. Say whether you approve or disapprove of things like
a) selling cigarettes to children
b) allowing teenagers to smoke
c) smoking in public places   *d*) blowing smoke in other people's faces, etc.

Interaction

You work for a small newspaper. Stapatski came to your town last night to give one of his 'concerts'. Since you personally cannot bear his kind of music, but have to write an article about it, you asked a friend to go instead. This is the information he gives you. *What are the questions you would have to ask to get it?*

The concert took place in Ronny Coward's 'Night Spot'. About 2,500 people were there. The cheapest ticket cost £5 and the most expensive £50. Stapatski played his own version of 'The Moonlight Sonata', 'Eine Kleine Nachtmusik' and 'Air on a G String' as well as a collection called 'Great Tunes from Great Operas'. The audience seemed to love every minute of it. Stapatski's fee for the night was said to be around £5000.

Summary

Use these notes to write *two* paragraphs summarising how Stapatski began his career and what he now does in his performances.

Paragraph 1
born – brought up New York. conservatory there. piano recitals – small towns. One evening – Wisconsin – audience bored – asked them what – . Someone – 'Old MacDonald'. – style – Chopin. audience – wild. Soon – night clubs.

Paragraph 2
Stapatski always – fancy clothes. glows – dark. silver and diamonds. also – three pianos. One – younger people. – coffin – motorcycle horn. The second – night clubs – diamonds. The third – friends. – mirror – spotlight.

Composition

Write between 150 and 200 words about one of these topics.

My idea of a good night's entertainment.   *or*

Which do you prefer – listening to music at home alone, or at concerts with other people? Why?

2.4a Football Hooliganism

 Michele Parks discusses the causes of the violent behaviour of football fans, and possible ways of preventing it. Her guests are Sir Cyril Brown, a Member of Parliament who frequently makes speeches about the 'break-down of Law and Order' and Christopher Marston, a sports journalist.

1

Parks: Sir Cyril, I know you have very strong views on the subject of football hooliganism.

Sir Cyril: Very strong, indeed. I am *sickened* and *disgusted* by the way so many football fans behave.

Parks: Could you give an example of the behaviour you have in mind.

Sir Cyril: There are hundreds of such examples!

Parks: Yes, but could you give us just one.

Sir Cyril: Very well. Think of last Saturday! A number of Manchester supporters found themselves on the same platform in a London tube station with a group of London fans. The London team had, I gather, just beaten the Manchester one. And what happened? There was a riot! The platform was wrecked. But far worse, forty people at least were seriously injured! That is only one example, and . . .

Parks: Before you go on, Sir Cyril, I wonder if I could ask Christopher Marston how he feels.

Marston: I . . . well . . . I'm certainly . . . deeply disturbed . . .

Sir Cyril: Disturbed? Disturbed? Only *disturbed*?

Marston: Let me go on! *All* violence is serious. But you say such violence is typical. And yet each Saturday during the season there are as many as forty-eight professional matches going on all over the country. Serious violence occurs at perhaps one or two of these matches. And it is always these examples that we read about, and not about all the other matches where there was no violence at all!

2

Parks: But why in your opinion does such violence occur at all? And how do you think it can be stopped?

What happened on the platform and what was the cause?

Now imagine you were on the platform. Describe to a friend what you saw and heard.

How, according to Marston, do people get the impression that such violence is typical?

2·4a

Why, according to Sir Cyril, does the violence occur? What do you think he believes ought to be done?

Sir Cyril: I am absolutely convinced that it is only one symptom of a general breakdown of Law and Order. And I am sure the main cause of this is the fact that the law itself has no teeth! When people are caught, they are let off far too lightly. Their punishment . . . if that's what it can be called . . . is usually a £25 fine and a lecture.

Marston: I'm not in favour simply of increasing fines and other forms of punishment. I'm more interested in prevention, and . . .

Sir Cyril: There's no doubt in my mind that . . .

Marston: How can you possibly *prevent* something by punishing people *after* they've done it?

Why does Marston disagree with Sir Cyril?

Sir Cyril: By showing others that they cannot get away with such things!

Marston: Fines and punishment haven't worked so far!

Sir Cyril: Only because they haven't been stiff enough!

Parks: How would *you* stop the violence, Christopher?

Do you think Marston's suggestion is a good one? Give reasons.

Marston: In my opinion the football clubs themselves must do something. For example, I would suggest banning anyone found guilty of violent behaviour from all football matches for a year.

3

Parks: I still don't think we've answered the question 'Why does such violence occur?'

Marston: I believe that one of the causes is boredom. People in their lives simply . . .

Sir Cyril: So now you're saying that football isn't exciting enough for the hooligans!

Explain what, in Marston's view, is the connection between boredom and violence at football matches.

Marston: Perhaps you'd let me make my point. I'm not saying that at all. What I *am* saying is too many people's lives are boring. For most of the week they lead dull, grey lives in offices or factories. Nothing they do has any importance. Football provides a cheap substitute for the drama and excitement that is lacking the rest of the time. They can shout, cheer and boo, . . . probably the only time they can do such things at all . . . and they can blow off steam . . . blow off all the aggression which they can't express the rest of the week.

Have you ever seen violent or very aggressive behaviour among spectators at a sporting event? Describe it.

Parks: Hmm. I'm still not sure we've found any answers or solutions, but thank you both very much.

2.4b

Text: comprehension and discussion

Multiple choice comprehension
Choose the *one* best answer: *a, b, c* or *d*.

1. According to Christopher Marston, football violence is *a)* not really serious at all *b)* caused only because people read about it *c)* serious but exaggerated by the newspapers *d)* more common than people realise.

2. Sir Cyril believes that the punishment is not *stiff* enough; that is, he thinks *a)* it can be changed too easily *b)* it has not been changed enough *c)* people do not know enough about it *d)* people should be punished more.

3. A *fine* is *a)* something you get for being good *b)* money you have to pay when you break the law *c)* the last words said in an interview *d)* the last part of a football match.

4. When Marston begins speaking about boredom among football fans, Sir Cyril *a)* does not really understand his point *b)* agrees that football is no longer exciting enough *c)* understands but disagrees *d)* says nothing at all.

5. Excitement is *lacking*. In other words, *a)* there is too much of it *b)* there is not enough of it *c)* people are getting less of it than before *d)* people are getting more of it than before.

6. When people *blow off steam*, they *a)* take off some of their clothes *b)* show they dislike something *c)* make a lot of noise *d)* get rid of nervous energy and tension.

Discussion

Describe some of the ways in which you personally 'blow off steam'.

Can you suggest any ways of preventing things like football violence?

Related practice

Opinions/proposals

Here are only three of the many ways of giving opinions or making proposals

In my opinion it would/would not be a good idea to...
As far as I'm concerned, we should...
I personally am/am not in favour of ...ing

In one sentence state your opinion about the following things.

Example
increasing fines for hooliganism
Answers
I'm not in favour of increasing fines for hooliganism
In my opinion it would be a good idea to increase fines for hooliganism

And what do you think of *a)* banning hooligans from all matches for a year *b)* making hooligans pay for the damage they cause *c)* giving hooligans lectures *d)* shooting hooligans in public *e)* fining anybody who boos or shouts at football matches.

Now think of some more things you are in favour of or against!

Describing how you feel about the way other people behave

Carefully study the simple construction below

I don't like I'm sickened by I really like He is upset by	the way	you speak the fans behave they act they are treated

Make sentences of your own expressing your feelings about the way *a)* your mother or someone else cooks *b)* prices are rising *c)* some people drive *d)* other people treat animals or children *e)* Sir Cyril talks about hooligans *f)* Marston talks about them *g)* young people dress.

2·4c

Further practice

Getting people's opinions

Note the change in structure in the second question

Why does the violence break out?

Why do you think the violence breaks out?

Make the same change. Begin each of these questions with 'Why do you think . . . ?' *a)* Why do fans riot? *b)* Why did the riot in the tube station occur? *c)* Why weren't the guilty ones punished? *d)* Why were they let off so lightly? *e)* Why don't the police stop them? *f)* Why didn't they stop the tube station riot?

Note some of the other ways of getting people's opinion.

What **in your opinion can be done to** stop such things?

What **do you think** is **the best way** to stop such things?

How in your opinion can such things be stopped?

Can you **propose/suggest some way of stopping** such things?

Now use these forms in order to get someone else's opinion about
a) catching hooligans *b)* punishing them *c)* preventing riots at football matches *d)* improving methods of teaching English.

Now think of some other things you would like other people's opinion on. Use the ways above or others to get it.

Reporting proposals

Christopher Marston said 'Hooligans should be banned from football matches for a year'.

In reporting this, you could say

He proposed banning hooligans from football matches for a year

In the same way, report these proposals.

Fines should be increased
The punishment should be made stiffer
Hooligans should be put in prison
They should be fined
Football matches should be stopped as soon as violence starts

Now report other proposals you have heard for preventing violence or punishing people. Always begin: 'Someone proposed . . .'

Interaction

You are talking to someone who happened to be in the London tube station when the riot described by Sir Cyril began. What are the questions you would ask to find out about *a)* the mood the Manchester fans were in (their team had lost) *b)* how the riot began and who was responsible *c)* the injuries done to the people and the damage done to the station *d)* what happened when the police came. Give the answers as well!

Summary

Summarise the main arguments put forward by both Sir Cyril and Christopher Marston about the cause of football hooliganism and its prevention. These questions may help you.

What did Sir Cyril think about the ways such hooligans are punished at present?
In what way did he think stiffer punishment would help prevent such things?
Why was Christopher Marston not in favour of this?
What was he in favour of?
Why did he think people with boring lives often became violent and aggressive at football matches?

Composition

Write between 150 and 200 words about one of these topics.

The importance of playing some kind of sport rather than just watching it.
or

Describe what you consider to be a typically 'dull and boring' job.

60

2·5a WHITE DEATH

 Michele Parks talks to an expert on sharks, Charles Kling, and a diver and underwater photographer, Ray Laster. Kling has written a book on sharks, and Laster has actually been attacked by one, and is still alive to tell the tale.

1

Imagine you were in that crowd on that beach, and a shark really attacked and ate a swimmer in front of your eyes. Describe what you saw, heard, felt and did.

What is not 'quite correct'?

Describe what you think happened off the Scottish coast not long ago.

Describe what sharks do when the water reaches about 18 degrees centigrade.

Parks: I saw a film recently in which a huge shark attacks a young girl and eats her alive. There's a crowd of people on a beach only a stone's throw away. Charles Kling... can such things really happen?

Kling: It depends where you are, of course, but in places like Australia, certain parts of Africa, and even the coast of Florida, such things *do* happen every year.

Parks: Well, luckily they can't happen here.

Kling: That isn't quite correct. As a matter of fact, they *can*! Sharks are seen fairly frequently off the English coast ... the Atlantic coast in particular. And not long ago, off the Scottish coast, one attacked a swimmer and ripped off his leg.

Parks: Really? I always thought... I mean, I was under the impression that sharks attack human beings only in warm conditions ... in the Pacific or the Caribbean, for instance ... that is, somehow I was sure that...

Kling: No. In point of fact, sharks attack in much colder conditions. But it *is* true, of course, that they're *more likely* to attack when the water temperature reaches about 18 degrees centigrade. They become hungrier then, and come much closer to shore, looking for food.

2

Parks: Ray Laster. Tell us about your experience.

Laster: Well... about ten years ago I was doing some underwater photography off the Australian coast. I was just about to come up and get into the boat when suddenly this ... huge shark came out of nowhere and sank its choppers ... you know ... teeth ... into me.

Parks: You must have been terrified. I mean, weren't you frightened out of your wits?

2.5a

Imagine you were in the small boat waiting for Laster to come out of the water just when the shark attacked him. Describe what you saw and did.	*Laster:* I ... I go white with fear when I think about it now, ... but strange as it may seem, at the time I was just ... dazed. I mean, I hardly realised what was happening. *Parks:* But surely you were in terrific pain! *Laster:* No, you may find this hard to believe but I felt almost nothing. If anything I felt ... sick. *Parks:* And how in the world did you get away?
Explain how and why Laster managed to get away from the shark.	*Laster:* Well, you see, the shark had bitten into my shoulder and chest and half my arm was actually sticking down its throat! And so it couldn't bite or swallow properly. With my free arm I managed to hit it hard on the snout ... nose ... and I stuck a finger in its eye. Suddenly it just let go. When they pulled me into the boat I was bleeding like a stuck pig but luckily I was all in one piece!

3

	Parks: Charles Kling. How intelligent are sharks? *Kling:* Oh, they have very tiny brains! *Parks:* And what's their strongest sense? *Kling:* They can smell even a tiny drop of blood half a kilometre away. *Parks:* In other words, it's their sense of smell.
Describe the sorts of things sharks can do well. What are the things they do not do very well? What does he mean by 'It might help to pray'? Do you think he is really serious?	*Kling:* Yeah, and they're also very sensitive to vibrations ... from a swimmer or a ship, for example. *Parks:* And their eyes? *Kling:* It may surprise you but they have a very poor sense of sight. They're even colour-blind. *Parks:* And what should we do if attacked by one? *Kling:* Try to kick or hit them in the eyes or on the snout. And if you're religious, it might help to pray.

2.5b

Text: comprehension and discussion

Multiple choice comprehension
Choose the *one* best answer: *a, b, c* or *d*.

1 What happened in the film after the girl was attacked by the shark? *a)* it killed her *b)* she threw a stone at it and escaped *c)* it ripped off her leg *d)* a crowd of people saved the girl's life.

2 According to Charles Kling *a)* sharks like attacking people in warm water conditions *b)* shark attacks happen most often in warm water conditions *c)* sharks never attack near the shore *d)* sharks usually attack near the shore.

3 How did Laster feel when he was attacked? *a)* absolutely terrified *b)* so surprised he could hardly believe it *c)* sick in his stomach but beside that he felt almost nothing at all *d)* ready to fight hard with the shark.

4 How badly was he hurt? *a)* A lot of blood was lost and that was all. *b)* He lost part of his arm. *c)* The shark bit off part of his shoulder. *d)* Half his arm and shoulder were bitten off.

5 Sharks are *sensitive to vibrations*. In other words, they *a)* enjoy moving a lot in the water *b)* can feel even small movements a long way away *c)* they do not sense movements very well *d)* they become angry if you move a lot.

6 According to Kling, when sharks attack *a)* you should hit them in the eyes only *b)* you should hit them in both eyes and nose *c)* there is nothing you can do at all *d)* you can only pray.

Discussion
Recently, there have been many 'disaster' films that show terrible things such as a yoing girl being eaten alive by a shark. How do you yourself feel about such films? Why do you think they are so popular?

Related practice

Saying things you think people may not believe

As strange as it may sound . . .
It may surprise you, but . . .
You may find this hard to believe, but . . .

Use one of these forms to tell someone else that you are sure you *a)* saw a ghost yesterday *b)* can speak 12 languages perfectly *c)* can see a shark in the swimming pool *d)* have a friend who has a shark as a pet *e)* aren't afraid of sharks at all.

Can you think of other things people might not believe? What are they? Talk about them!

Correcting people

Notice what Kling says here.

Parks: Well, luckily there are no sharks off our coast.
Kling: **As a matter of fact, there are!**

Note the stress here on *are*.
Now correct Parks in the same way when she says

Luckily sharks don't attack people here
No sharks have ever attacked people here!
People can be sure of being safe in British waters
British sharks wouldn't attack people
Our sharks are peaceful!
What you say just isn't so!

Describing fear, terror, etc.

I was frightened out of my wits I was absolutely terrified I went white with fear	when . . .

Make 5 or 6 sentences of your own using these. Think of things that really terrify you to put after *when* . . .

2.5c

Further practice

Expressing opinions you suspect may be wrong

This happens more often than we realise. Almost as we say something, we become aware that it is probably wrong.

But I was under the impression that...
Really? I thought that...
But somehow I was sure that...
You mean, it isn't true that...

Suppose you are Michele Parks. How would you say that you suspect the following opinions may be wrong?

Sharks attack only in warm water
There are no man-eating sharks around Britain
Such things happen only in Australia
British swimmers are completely safe
Such things could never happen here
Man-eating sharks are found only in the Pacific
We have nothing to worry about

Now suppose you are in the following situations. What would you say?

Your teacher tells you you got a bad mark in the last examination. You were sure it was a good one.

Your dentist tells you all your teeth must come out. You thought they were all in a very good condition.

A mechanic tells you your car is not safe. You can't believe it.

Someone tells you the lake you are swimming in has got sharks in it. You are very surprised.

Interaction

You are in a public swimming pool. Ray Laster is also swimming there. You notice his scars (the marks left by the shark that attacked him). Ask him questions beginning a) How
b) When   c) Was it very painful?
d) What do you remember about the moment when...? e) But how in the world did you...? f) You mean you really...?

Word formation

Find the correct form of the word on the left so that it can be used on the right.

frequent   I have ___ seen sharks here
likely   What is the ___ of a shark attack in water like this?
photograph   Laster was an expert in underwater ___
believe   Such things are beyond ___
blood   Laster was ___ badly when he got back into the boat
intelligent   Sharks have very little ___
colour-blind   They suffer from ___
pray   Say a ___ for me!
see   Sharks have very poor ___

Summary

Summarise what Charles Kling says about sharks and Ray Laster's experience with one. The summary should concentrate on these points

Where can shark attacks occur? Under what sort of conditions are they most likely?

Where was Ray Laster attacked? How did he escape? What did he feel at the time?

What do you learn about the intelligence, sense of smell and sight and sensitivity to vibration of sharks?

What would you do if attacked by one?

Composition

Write between 150 and 200 words about one of these topics.

Describe a frightening situation you have been in, with a large, angry dog or on a lonely, dark street, for example.
or
Describe a terrifying film you have seen.

Section Three *Listening Comprehension*

This is a very special section. It is very different from the other two.

What you will hear about

In this section you will hear, and not read, passages about such things as

an escape from a prison

a man with two wives and lives

a girl, a rather foolish dog, and how they stop two criminals

a writer who grows up during one war, sees his friends killed in another, and who finally wins a famous prize for his books

a lot of people who almost get killed

a room you would hate to live in

a girl who perhaps would not take a job offered to her if she knew more about it

the end of a very difficult journey.

What this section contains

This section has ten Units of Material. Each Unit has two pages. There are various things in each Unit, like pictures for discussion and interpretation; comprehension exercises on the passage you have heard; use of English exercises; vocabulary and composition work.

The passages themselves are not printed in the Units. They are all in the booklet inserted into the back of the book. They may be taken out and given to you later.

This section deals with the skills of

Listening comprehension (Paper 4); Interpreting pictures and photographs (Paper 5); Use of English (Paper 3). And, of course, you will continue to get general practice in using English communicatively. For example, among other things, you will learn ways of

showing *different* degrees of certainty

expressing surprise and astonishment

showing anger at the way other people treat you

complaining

making metaphors and similes

expressing gratitude and appreciation

calming people, reassuring them

showing disappointment

criticising people, suggesting that they have made mistakes

Suggestions to the teacher

Presenting the passages for listening comprehension
(Units 3.1 to 3.6)

This is the suggested presentation procedure for the first six units in this section

The passages themselves are in the booklet inserted into the back of the book. Since in the examination your students will never actually see the passage read to them by the examiner, you may wish to remove these passages from the books before they are distributed to the class.

Or, if the students buy the books privately, you can ask them to give you these passages. The passages can then either *a)* be given back at the end of the course *b)* be given back individually each time one is read.

The presentation procedure itself is *a)* discuss the lead-in picture that begins each unit *b)* focus attention on the general comprehension questions *c)* read aloud, or play the recording of the text at least once *d)* see if the class can answer the questions *e)* then play the passage a second time and move on to the more detailed comprehension or summary questions afterwards *f)* do the remaining exercises.

The last *four* Units (3.7, 3.8, 3.9, 3.10) are slightly different.

Presenting passages 3.7 to 3.10

The first six Units are specially designed as a *preparation* for the listening comprehension part of the examination.

For example, the picture itself always relates directly to the story. The first set of *Related practice* questions give some clue also as to what the passage is about, and help orient general comprehension.

However, the last four passages approximate far more closely to the actual tasks of the examination. For example *a)* the photograph relates only to the general theme of the passage; it is now designed to promote exactly the same skills required for Paper 5 *b)* the listening comprehension itself is exactly the same in form as in the paper; that is, between 5 and 6 multiple-choice questions have to be answered.

The other exercises

These vary in type and purpose. All exercises that are labelled *Use of English* are specially suited for homework as well as oral work in class. Some composition exercises are also given, though this is much less stressed in this section than in others. The other exercises are primarily oral ones, suited for use in the classroom itself.

Escape from Hanley Park

Look at the picture and discuss

Describe what you think is happening and what the people you see are trying to do.

Where do you think the scene is taking place?

Look at the rope ladder. Think of various ways it might have got there.

Listening comprehension and related practice

General comprehension
Listen to the passage with these questions in mind. It is from a radio news programme.

What exactly is 'Hanley Park'?
How many men got away from it?
What happened to one of the men?

Multiple choice comprehension
Listen to the passage a second time. As you do so, tell the teacher to stop reading (or the tape) when you think you have heard the answer to a question. Repeat or summarise the information you have heard.

1 On the other side of the wall, there is *a)* a smaller exercise yard *b)* a kind of park *c)* an ordinary street *d)* a furniture shop.
2 The escape began when some men *a)* climbed through a hole in the prison roof *b)* climbed the wall from the other side *c)* began to fight with prison guards *d)* forced guards to give them two ladders.
3 When the ladders were lowered *a)* a group of prisoners ran to them immediately *b)* the men from the other side climbed down *c)* a group of prisoners was waiting there *d)* a second group of prisoners informed the guards about them.
4 The information about the man in hospital *a)* was definitely given the reporter by the police *b)* is probably true even though the police have not said so *c)* is probably false *d)* comes from the hospital

Vocabulary
1 It was a *daring* escape; that is, it *a)* happened during the day *b)* was well-organised *c)* was successful *d)* took a lot of courage and imagination to do.
2 The men *apparently* climbed through a hole in the roof of the lorry. In other words *a)* everybody saw them do it *b)* as far as is known this is what happened *c)* it was hard for them to do this *d)* the story is untrue.
3 Some of the prisoners *rioted*. They *a)* began shouting and fighting *b)* ran very fast *c)* got hurt *d)* refused to help.

Interaction
You are a reporter talking to prison officials about the escape. You know only that at least one prisoner got away. Ask questions to find out *a)* the time of the escape *b)* if it is true a lorry of some kind was involved *c)* where the lorry was and what part it played

3.1

d) where the prisoners were at the time   e) exactly how many got away   f) how the guards managed to stop the others   g) if anyone was hurt   h) how he got hurt   i) about his injuries   j) where he is now.

Use of English 1
Supply any word or words you think necessary to complete this article.

DARING PRISON ESCAPE
It has now been definitely (1) by the police that a man (2) in escaping (3) Birmingham's Hanley Park Prison yesterday and that a second man was badly hurt (4) attempting (5) so. This second man is said (6) from one of the two ladders (7) in the escape. The escape is understood to (8) executed (9) the help of a gang that specialises (10) men out of prison and which has been (11) in similar escape plots in (12) countries (13) in Europe but in North and South America as well. Although the name of the man who escaped has not yet been (14) by prison authorities, it is widely (15) that he is none (16) Basil King, who three years (17) was (18) of murdering his millionaire playboy friend, Nigel Woods and (19) to 10 years (20) prison. King is 35 years (21), 6 feet (22) and (23) around 80 kilos. He has several scars (24) his face, one of (25) has the (26) of an 'S'. It is on his right (27) just below his eye.

Use of English 2
Finish each sentence so that it means the same more or less as the one above.

It is known that one man got away.
One man is known . . .

It is said that another is in hospital.
Another is said . . .

Our reporter asked the police 'Is he badly hurt?'
Our reporter asked the police if . . .

The police would neither confirm nor deny this.
The police refused . . .

'However, order has now been restored in the prison!' they confirmed.
They confirmed that . . .

Expressing suppositions rather than definite facts

One prisoner is **understood to be** in hospital. Another is **supposed to have got** away. Police are **said to be looking** for a large green lorry now.

Study the sentences above. Observe not only the three different ways used to express suppositions (understood/supposed/said) but also how time is indicated (to be . . . to have done, to be . . . ing). Now make these statements of fact into expressions of supposition.
The escape was well-organised.
One prisoner is badly hurt.
The other is hiding in Birmingham.
The police know who organised it.
One man has tried to escape before.
Several people are already helping the police with their investigation.
Only one man actually got away.

In the same way, talk about a 'famous person' (real or imaginary) or persons about whom there are a lot of 'stories'.

Open-ended dialogue
The man who got away was Basil King. You have just seen him in a restaurant. You are phoning the police.
Policeman: James Street Station.
You: ___
Policeman: Basil King? Are you sure?
You: ___
Policeman: Just a moment. I'll put you through to C.I.D.
CID Man: C.I.D. Can I help you?
You: ___
CID Man: How can you be sure? I mean, please describe this man to us.
You: ___
CID Man: You know, sir, we get lots of calls like this. Are you joking?
You: ___

3·2 A DOUBLE LIFE

Look at the picture and discuss

Where do you think this scene is taking place? Give reasons for your answer.

Look at the two women with their children. Who do you think they might be?

Why do you think the man is looking so tired and frightened? Give some possible explanations.

Listening comprehension and related practice

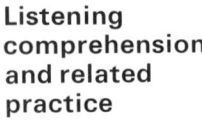

General comprehension

Listen to the passage with these questions in mind. Then answer them.

In what sense has the man been leading a 'double life'?
What finally put an end to this?
The word 'bigamy' is used in the passage. What does it mean?

Multiple choice

Listen to the passage a second time. When you can answer a question, tell the teacher to stop. Repeat or summarise the information you heard.

1 At the beginning of his first marriage, Harrison a) could not settle down to marriage at all b) had terrible nightmares c) immediately became a bad husband and father d) was a very good husband and father.
2 In this period of his marriage he a) had to travel a lot because of his job b) had problems in finding a job at all c) was unhappy when his job was taken away d) pretended to have a job as a lorry driver.
3 The second woman in his life was a woman a) he had fallen in love with before b) whose first husband was dead c) who was still married as well d) who knew about his first wife.
4 Harrison lived his two lives a) in the same suburb b) in different parts of the same city c) in different countries d) in different parts of the same country.
5 He collapsed because a) both wives had children at the same time b) he had to work so hard c) both wives found out about him d) a doctor discovered his double life.
6 The police found out about him because a) he decided to tell them b) one of his wives told them c) he made several foolish mistakes and the police found out by themselves d) his doctor advised them to arrest him.
7 His punishment is that he a) will go to prison for at least two years b) can go free as long as he does not do the same thing again over the next four years c) may have to stay in prison for six years d) will go to prison for four years.

Vocabulary

Give the missing word or words

Her husband is dead. She is a ___.

He really loves his family. He is a ___ family man.

3·2

The police did not have to catch him; he ___ himself ___.

He was given a sentence but will not have to serve it unless he gets into trouble again. His sentence was ___.

He said he was guilty in court. He ___ ___.

Interaction

You are the doctor that Harrison comes to with his problems. All you know about him so far is that he is obviously overworked. Work out a dialogue with him based on these points

You ask about his main job. He tells you.

You find out if he has any part-time jobs. He tells you he has (as a painter, taxi driver, mechanic on Sundays and professional baby sitter).

You ask why he has so many jobs. He decides to tell you about his two wives.

You express great surprise and ask how long this has been going on. He tells you.

You inquire about the number of children he has to support, and if they are all his.

He tells you everything and asks for advice. At first you cannot think of any. You are still too surprised.

Finally you advise him to give himself up. At first he does not want to, and then accepts your advice.

Use of English 1

Use these notes to write a full summary of the Harrison case. Be sure to join sentences with connectors like

When   However   Then   Finally During this period   etc.

first married – Harrison – devoted family man.
job – away – long periods.
a widow named Claudia Paisley – a double life – five years ago.
different jobs – support his two families.
a mental and physical collapse – a doctor – give himself up.
guilty – bigamy – suspended sentence – two years.

Surprise and astonishment

I can't imagine how he managed to get away with it for so long.
I'm very surprised that he was able to get away with it at all.
I mean, how in the world did he manage to hide the truth from his two wives?

These are just a few of the ways used to express great surprise. Note not only such phrases as 'I can't imagine how . . .' and 'How in the world . . .' but also the use of 'managed to' and 'was able to'.

Now express great surprise at the fact that Harrison   a) worked 20 hours a day   b) drove a lorry as well   c) kept both wives happy   d) supported two families   e) lived normal lives with both of them.

Now talk about other things in the Harrison case that surprise you. Also use 'I just can't understand why he/they didn't . . .' and 'I find it really surprising that he/they never . . .'

Use of English 2

Report these things Harrison said.

Begin each of your sentences as shown.

Example

'I'm a bigamist.' He admitted . . .

Answer

He admitted that he was a bigamist.

'I've got two wives.' He confessed . . .
'I won't try to escape.' He promised . . .
'Life in prison is probably better than my life now.' He thought . . .
'Will the judge give me a long sentence?' He asked . . .
'What's the usual sentence for bigamy?' He wanted to know . . .
'Don't send me back to my two wives.' He begged the police . . .

3·3 Prince Albert and the Jewel Robbers

Look at the picture and discuss

What do you think has happened here? Try to imagine different possibilities.

Do you really think it is possible that the girl in the picture could have fought the two men and beaten them? If so, how?

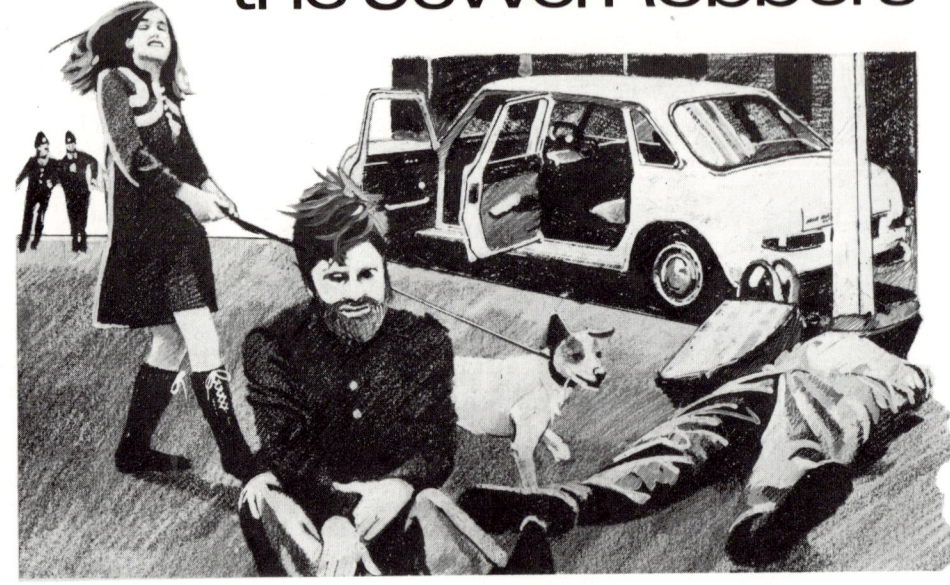

Listening comprehension and related practice

General comprehension

Who, or what, is Prince Albert?

Why did the man in the car get angry with the girl, and what did he do?

How did it happen that the other man was knocked unconscious?

Detailed comprehension

Listen to the passage again. Answer the questions as you go along.

1 Describe some of the things Linda had done in order to make friends.
2 What do you learn about her job?
3 Describe Prince Albert.
4 Where was Linda going that morning and why was Prince Albert with her?
5 Why do you think Prince Albert was so interested in the lamp post?
6 Describe the car and the man in it.
7 Describe what the man said and Linda did before the other man came.
8 Now explain exactly how the other man was knocked unconscious.
9 Explain in what way Linda found her judo useful.
10 How do you think the policemen felt when they saw what had happened?
11 Why do you think they felt this way?
12 Explain what happened then.

Vocabulary

Choose the *one* best word or phrase that you think explains the underlined words.

1 Prince was a <u>mongrel</u>. He was a dog that *a)* looked strange *b)* could not control itself *c)* was no one definite type of dog *d)* did not like strangers.
2 Prince was <u>on a lead,</u> or in other words *a)* out for a walk *b)* loaned to Linda only for a short time *c)* could smell something strange around the lamp post *d)* had a collar round his neck and was tied to some kind of line.
3 He <u>sniffed</u> round the lamp post, or *a)* felt it *b)* ran round it *c)* smelt round it *d)* got the lead twisted round it.
4 The lead got <u>entangled</u> round the man's feet. In other words, it was *a)* wrapped round them *b)* broken *c)* pulled from Linda's hand *d)* dropped round them.
5 He fell <u>with a thud.</u> In other words he *a)* did not want to fall *b)* tried to stop himself falling *c)* hit the ground or lamp post with a loud sound *d)* could not be heard.

6 The policemen gaped, or a) jumped out b) looked carefully c) began to laugh d) stared in great surprise.
7 One of the men was sprawled on the pavement. In other words he was a) badly hurt b) lying there with his arms and legs sticking out c) trying to get up d) thrown back by one of the policemen.
8 He was winded, or a) without any breath left b) wrapped round the lamp post c) tied up d) very angry.

Use of English
Supply the missing word or words to finish this newspaper article about Linda.

GIRL BEATS UP JEWEL ROBBERS
The police could hardly (1) their eyes. There, in front of them, were the two men who had been (2) in a daring jewel (3) only a few seconds (4) . One of them was hurt so badly that he could hardly (5) to his feet. The second lay on the pavement (6) a sack of potatoes. And (7) had (8) all this? A young woman who had (9) a few judo lessons (10) a sports club!

The girl, Linda Freeman, who (11) from a small village near Newcastle-on-Tyne later (12) reporters exactly (13) it had all (14) .

'I was on my (15) to the supermarket (16) my dog, Prince. Prince suddenly stopped (17) a lamp post. There was a car (18) next to it, and a man inside it (19) me to (20) off! He (21) some very insulting language as well! Just then another man (22) round the corner and shouted at me to (23) away from the car. Prince barked at him and (24) between him and the lamp post. I (25) Prince on a lead and somehow the lead became (26) round the man's feet. As a (27) , he (28) against the lamp post and (29) himself unconscious.

'I (30) down to help the man. But (31) the man in the car jumped out and tried to (32) me out of the (33) . I thought he was trying to (34) me, and so I (35) him (36) my shoulder.'

Interaction
You are one of the policemen who arrive just after Linda has thrown the driver of the car over her shoulder. What questions would you ask (and what do you think would be the answers) to find out a) if she has ever seen the men before b) what she was doing near the car at all c) how she managed to throw one man over her shoulder d) how and why she learned Judo e) how she managed to knock the other man unconscious.

Showing anger at the way other people treat you

If someone starts swearing at you, you might say a number of things, among them

**You have no right to swear at me like that!
How dare you swear at me like that!
Who do you think you are to swear at me like that?**

Use one or more of these to show anger because someone is a) pushing you about b) shouting at you c) insulting you d) ordering you to do things e) treating you like a dog.

Think of some other things people could do that would make you very angry. What would you say?

Composition/discussion
You know someone like Linda who comes from a small town and now lives in a very large one. This person is very lonely. What advice would you give him or her about how to make friends and what kind of people to avoid?

After discussing this, put the advice in the form of a letter to a 'lonely friend in a big city' (150–200 words).

3.4 The Prize 1

Look at the picture and discuss

What do you think is about to happen?

Look at these dates. Give reasons either for or against saying this scene happened at or around these times
a) 55 BC   b) 1350
c) 1914–18.

How would you feel if you were one of those soldiers?

Listening comprehension and related practice

General comprehension
Listen to the passage with these questions in mind. In it, a famous writer talks about his youth.

What has the scene above to do with the passage?

What happened to the author's father?

What do we learn about his mother?

Detailed comprehension
Listen to the passage again. Ask the teacher to stop reading (or the tape) when you think you can answer a question or do part of the task fully.

1 Make sentences about the author using the words below
small town – West of England – father – journalist – First World War – eleven.
2 Describe what he remembers about his father.
3 Talk about the author's memories of school and in particular   a) the teachers   b) the food   c) the Latin and Greek lessons.
4 Explain what 'Passchendale' was and what happened there.
5 What happened in 1919?
6 What do we learn about the author's aunt?
7 Would you say he liked her? Give reasons for your answer!

Express these ideas with words or phrases from the passage

The author spent his youth in the town. He ___ ___ there.

His father liked to laugh and could see the funny side of life. He had a ___ ___ ___.

Two armies fought at Passchendale. It was a big ___.

A great number of people had influenza at the same time. In other words, there was an influenza ___.

It was his aunt and not his parents who took care of him when he was young. He was ___ ___ his aunt.

Interaction
You are talking to the author in a pub. Like other old men, he likes 'remembering things'. Work out questions with these words, and then his answers.

Example
Remember your father very well?

Question
Can you remember your father very well?

Answer
No, not really. You see, he . . . (etc.)

a) father's job?   b) remember anything about him?   c) remember about school? *d)* like the teachers very much? *e)* where – when – father killed? *f)* a very bad battle? *g)* mother still alive? *h)* raised you? *i)* like your aunt very much?

Use of English – word formation
The word in italics on the left can be used in a *different form* to complete the sentence on the right. For example

remember This is about the author's ___ of the war.
Answer **memories**

enormous My father must have loved my mother ___.
hear I can remember ___ them laughing.
laugh I heard their ___ coming from the kitchen.
mean My school work had no ___. meaning; in other words, it was
translate We had to do ___ from the Greek and Latin classics.
classic Since then I have always hated ___ studies.
religion I was raised by a very ___ aunt.
blood My father died in one of the ___ battles of the war.

Suppositions about the past
What are the missing words here?

He must have ___ a pleasant man.
My mother must ___ loved him very much.

Use '... must have (done)' to respond to this old man. The words in brackets can be used in part of the response. For example –
Old Man: School was boring! Oh, when I think about it! (hate, terrible)
You: **You must have hated it!**
or **It must have been terrible.**

And now the old man is saying:

My father loved jokes and laughter! (a good sense of humour. pleasant man)

In school we had to do a lot of meaningless translations! (bored)

Passchendale was one of the bloodiest battles of the war! (terrible. A lot of soldiers – die)

During the war there was never enough to eat. (very hungry. very weak)

After the war a lot of people died from influenza. (terrible epidemic)

I had it, too. I was very thin and hungry but somehow I survived. (lucky)

After the war I heard about my father. It seems he was wounded, and fell into a hole full of water. He died there. (drown. A lot of others – the same way)

Complaining – showing that you don't understand the point of things
The author thought that doing translations from Homer was meaningless. He could have said at the time (to one of his teachers)

I really don't see why we have to do these translations!
Excuse me, but what's the point of doing these translations?
In what way will doing these translations help us?

Use these constructions to show that you think the following things are meaningless *a)* doing this exercise. *b)* reading this book *c)* answering all these questions *d)* writing all these compositions *e)* doing summaries *f)* learning all these words.

Composition and/or discussion
Think back to your own school days when you were perhaps 12 or 14. What were the things that seemed rather meaningless to you? What, on the other hand, seemed useful and good? How would you do things differently if you were the teacher?

3.5 The Prize 2

Look at the picture and discuss

When or where could this scene have occurred?

Describe what is happening.

What will the men in the bomber have to do in order to save themselves?

Listening comprehension and related practice

General comprehension
In this passage, the famous writer in *The Prize (1)* talks about a later period of his life. As you listen keep these questions in mind and answer them at the end.
Where and around which time did the scene actually occur?
How did the author feel as he watched?
What happened to the men in the plane?

Detailed comprehension
Listen to the passage again. This time ask the teacher to stop reading (or the tape) when you think you can answer a question fully.

1 Make sentences about the author using the words below.
Second World War – abroad a great deal – two years – German university – journalist – Far East – Japan – a great many friends
2 Explain what you think he means when he says 'It was as if a black curtain had been drawn between them and me'.
3 Ask and answer questions about the author at the time of the scene he describes. Use these words
a) Where b) When c) Why.
4 The author mentions a town 'further up the river'. Describe what was happening there and what the author could see and hear.
5 Now describe what happened 'shortly afterwards'. Use these words in full sentences as you do so.
warned – coming our way – engines – searchlights criss-crossed – above us – guns – fire – flame. The anti-aircraft crew – cheer.
6 The author did not cheer himself. Explain why.
7 He later mentions 'other friends' in 'different bombers'. Explain just who you think these people were.

Multiple choice vocabulary
Choose the *one* word you think best completes the sentence.

1 The author had __ a lot of experience of working and living abroad.
a) done b) made c) had d) taken.
2 The mouth of a river is where the river __ into the sea.
a) streams b) flows c) stretches d) waters.
3 A town was being bombed. An air-__ was going on.
a) raid b) battle c) bombing d) drop.

4 He saw a flicker of flame. It was still not really very___
   a) loud b) light c) bright d) strong.
5 For a moment, the scene___him as unreal.
   a) hit b) seemed c) regarded d) struck.
6 It suddenly___to the author that he might know some of the men in the plane.
   a) fell into b) arrived c) occurred d) happened.
7 The bomber was ___ down and crashed.
   a) shot b) knocked c) fired d) hit.
8 All the crew died. Nobody ___ the crash.
   a) got over b) got through c) survived d) withstood.

Interaction
You are talking to the author about the experience described in the passage. You are really interested now in his feelings at the time rather than what he saw. Using questions like

**What exactly were your feelings when . . .
Can you describe how you felt when . . .
How did you feel about the fact that . . .**

ask him about the moment when he
a) heard the bombers coming over
b) heard the guns firing   c) realised he might be killed himself   d) saw one of the bombers burst into flame
e) realised some of his friends might be in the plane   f) saw no parachutes.

   Try to imagine possible answers to these questions as well. Rather than describe what you think the author felt, describe what you think *you* would have felt if you had been there. Some of the terms you may find useful in describing your feelings are

terrified/shaking with fear/horrified/sickened/so confused I hardly knew what was happening.

Prepositions
Give the missing prepositions in this article written after the raid.

London, Dec 21, 1941
Last night there were air raids (1) Dover, Folkestone as well (2) Gravesend and other targets (3) the Thames.
   Bombs were also dropped (4) other targets (5) the London area. According (6) official sources, 25 enemy planes were shot down. The loss (7) our own air force has not yet been confirmed.

Metaphors/similes
These are ways of making comparisons between things, like

**The bombs sounded like huge kettle drums that were being tuned for a concert.
The plane looked like a fly that was caught in a spider's net.
I felt as if I were inside one of those drums.
It was rather like watching a film.**

Note particularly terms like
**looked/sounded like . . .
I felt as if I were . . .
It was rather like . . . ing . . .**

Now use these terms and others like

taste like . . ./smell like . . .
reminds me of . . .

in order to describe   a) a very bad meal   b) cheap, horrible wine or beer   c) a hot day in a city that has no parks or water anywhere   d) what you feel like after spending all night in a smoky room and perhaps after drinking too much as well   e) a house that is on fire and burning brightly   f) a very cold room without any heating at all   g) an underground train during the rush hour in London, New York or Tokyo.

Composition/discussion
Why do you think 'it is difficult to hate people whose names you know and whose language you speak,' etc. (between 50 and 150 words).

3.6 The Prize 3

Look at the picture and discuss

Who could these people be and why have they gathered?

What do you think has happened or is going to happen later?

How would you feel if you had to make a speech in front of all those people?

Listening comprehension and related practice

Multiple choice general comprehension

In this passage the author of the last two passages has just received an international literary prize. He has to make a speech. Listen to it with these questions in mind. Then, after you have heard it, choose the *one* best answer for each.

1 From what the author has said it would seem he has written books about   *a*) simple things for simple people   *b*) terrible things he has imagined   *c*) terrible things that have actually happened to him personally   *d*) the things he has observed and seen happen to other people.

2 He prefers simple language because *a*) this is what simple people can understand   *b*) complicated language is always a lie   *c*) the events he describes are simple and so the language must be so, too   *d*) it is the best way to describe things accurately and truthfully.

3 What he says also suggests that he believes   *a*) nobody can really be sure whether they are right or not   *b*) finding the truth is simple if you use simple language   *c*) people are not really interested in truth   *d*) he personally is always right.

General summaries

Now listen to the passage a second time. This time summarise all the information which you think leads you to answers for the questions on the left!

For example, if you have chosen answer *d*) for question 1, give the facts which you believe confirm that answer.

Detailed comprehension and interpretation

You may listen to the passage a third time or prefer to read it silently (see page 66). After doing so, try to answer these questions as fully as possible.

What kind of events do you think he has written about? Give examples of some of the actual things he might have written about.

Put the following sentences into 'simple' words which the author (and George Orwell) would prefer
This is a low-risk operation.
We are going to pacify that village.
It is an area of disorder.
All hostile villagers will be pacified.

Use these notes to summarise what the German writer said about the truth.
not the possession – sincere search – truly human. arrogant, proud and lazy if –.

Now explain why you think the author says he has tried to *'get at'* the truth in his books rather than *'know'* or *'find'* the truth.

Interaction
You are a member of an international prize-giving committee. Your committee has decided to give the author of this passage its prize for 'outstanding achievement in the field of literature and human relations'. There are two choices open to the author. He can either   *a*) be invited to accept the prize at a very formal and distinguished gathering in front of Kings, Queens, Prime Ministers, etc.; however in this case very little money will be given along with the prize or   *b*) be sent the prize through the post as well as all the money that would otherwise be spent on the formal gathering.

You are speaking to the author on the phone. Explain the choice to him. Work out the questions you would ask to find out which he prefers. Finally, ask more questions in order to find out his reasons for his choice. (Work out the answers, too. Which would you personally prefer? And why?)

Interpretation and discussion
Here are some more statements in rather complicated language. Try to express the same ideas in the sort of simpler language Orwell and the author suggest. Then discuss which version you think 'closer to the real truth'.

Yesterday evening, while under the unfortunate and temporary influence of alcohol, I used excessive physical force in an attempt to obtain money from several elderly people who happened to be passing by.

The directors of the international company that controls this factory have decided upon its immediate closure as a result of its low profitability. The directors regret any hardship to employees.

The train drivers' union has, in pursuit of its latest wage claim, been forced to adopt a policy of complete non co-operation with the management.

Expressing gratitude and appreciation (formal)
I wish to express my deep gratitude to you for . . . ing
I should like to thank you most sincerely for . . . ing
I/We deeply appreciate the fact that . . .

Use one or more of these forms for the following situations.

Someone has just given a speech to your club. You have to thank him or her.

You have just been given a prize for the 'best English essay by a foreign student' and have to make a very short speech.

An important foreign guest (whose language nobody speaks but who speaks English) has visited your school, office or factory. You have to say a 'few words of welcome'.

3·7 A SLIGHT EMERGENCY

Questions

Describe the scene in the photograph.

Describe what you think is happening *outside* the building.

What are some of the things you think the people in this picture are probably saying?

What do you think these people would do and say if they were suddenly told that all flights had just been cancelled?

Talking points

Advantages and disadvantages of air travel compared to rail/car/bus.

Describe all the things you have to do before going on a long journey.

Now describe a trip by air, rail or car which you have recently taken.

Listening comprehension and related practice

You are going to hear a passage about an incident during an airplane flight. Listen to the passage once or twice. Then answer the questions below and do the exercises on the next page.

1 The incident described here is caused when   *a)* a passenger suddenly starts shouting   *b)* an engine catches fire   *c)* the plane begins losing altitude fast   *d)* someone says the plane is going to crash.

2 When did the emergency occur?
a) we are not told   *b)* just before the plane landed in New York
c) shortly after the plane took off
d) sometime in the middle of the flight.

3 When the author saw the smoke and flames he   *a)* told the others to keep calm   *b)* demanded to know what was happening   *c)* became very very frightened   *d)* thought it was only a slight emergency.

4 During the emergency, the cabin crew   *a)* were very active and kept people calm   *b)* did hardly anything at all   *c)* looked very worried and upset   *d)* kept smiling brightly.

5 During the emergency, the old lady
a) kept talking about her relatives
b) just slept   *c)* seemed sure they were going to crash   *d)* felt very sick.

6 When they landed, she   *a)* was one of the first to get out   *b)* asked when they were going on to New York
c) was shaking violently with fear
d) was not even sure where they were.

Interaction

You are talking to the author of the passage a few days after the emergency. What questions would you ask to find out about   *a)* his feelings when he was first told the plane was returning to London   *b)* how he knew (and when) that something was really wrong   *c)* his own reaction and that of the other passengers   *d)* the actions of the cabin crew   *e)* the landing itself.

3·7

Vocabulary
Find the *one* best answer.

1 The old lady had been *chatty*. She had a) noticed nothing b) talked a lot c) been very calm d) wanted to sleep.
2 When you *reassure* people, you try to a) make them sit down b) speak more slowly c) pay more money d) make them feel safe, less afraid.
3 The stewardess's smile was *strained*. It was a) easy for her b) very hard c) something she was trained to do d) only a small smile.
4 The *bump* was probably caused by a) the engines roaring b) the plane losing altitude c) the wheels touching the ground very hard d) someone shouting.
5 The brakes *screeched*. They a) did not work b) worked very well c) made a loud noise d) could not be heard at all.

Use of English 1
Re-write each sentence with the beginning below it.

An old lady was sitting next to me.
There . . .

She fell asleep immediately after take-off.
As soon as . . .

'Are we going to crash?' someone asked.
Someone asked if . . .

'Don't get up' a stewardess told us.
We were told . . .

The brakes screeched. I could hear them.
I could hear . . .

'Surely the journey isn't over already?' the old lady said.
She could hardly . . .

Use of English 2
An American named Ken wrote an English girl named Alison a letter just before the plane took off. Reconstruct the letter from these notes.

plane – off – few minutes. Before – want to tell you – enjoyed week – with you – London! I – really looking forward – you – New York next year. – sure – you – like New York very much. I – you – all the interesting places there. hope you – letter soon.

Begin and end the letter in the way you think Ken would have done.

Telling people to do things in a calm, reassuring way

There's no need to . . .
Now, please don't . . .
Just . . . and everything will . . .

You are a member of the cabin-crew. Use one of these forms to tell people a) not to get nervous b) to stay calm c) to leave the plane quietly d) to stay in their seats e) not to worry too much f) not to fight when they slide out of the emergency exit g) follow your instructions exactly.

Dialogue composition
You were on the plane. Your mother is expecting you in New York now. But you are still in London. Explain to her a) why the plane returned to London b) what happened when you landed again. Be sure to reassure her. She is very upset by the news and is sure you must be hurt. Calm her down.

Do this orally first and then in writing.

3·8 THE ROOM

Questions

Describe the room in the picture.

Does it tell you anything about the person who lives in it? What?

Could this room belong to a *a)* middle-aged businessman *b)* young man working in a factory *c)* very old lady or man? Give reasons for each 'Yes' or 'No' answer.

Talking points

Describe the room, flat or house you live in.

What are the advantages of having a house as compared to a flat?

You have to rent a small flat for yourself. What are your requirements in regard to size, location, number of rooms, things you particularly want in it?

Listening comprehension

This passage is about a student named Jean who is looking for a room in London. Listen at least twice. Then answer the questions and do the exercises.

1 What are we told about the man who opened the door? *a)* He had been shaving when Jean knocked. *b)* He was not young and was shabby in appearance. *c)* He did not like strangers at all. *d)* He did not like Jean at all.
2 The house itself seemed to *a)* have a lot of small rooms *b)* be very clean and neat *c)* be a kind of restaurant, too *d)* have a lot of old people in it.
3 The man told her that the room *a)* had someone in it at that time *b)* had been vacant for some time *c)* was going to be cleaned soon *d)* had just been cleaned.
4 The room itself was *a)* comfortable but dusty *b)* part of the hallway *c)* well-furnished and clean *d)* small, dark and unpleasant.
5 Mr Cartwright was a man who *a)* had spoken to Jean before *b)* wanted to live in the room then *c)* was old and had died there *d)* had never really liked the room.

Interaction

You are a friend of Jean's. What questions would you ask her (and what are her answers) to find out about *a)* the man who opened the door *b)* the house itself *c)* the decoration of the room *d)* the furniture in it and other things.

Vocabulary

Choose the *one* best answer.

1 A room with nobody living in it is *a)* unlived *b)* free *c)* vacant *d)* left.
2 The money you pay for a room is called *a)* rent *b)* pension *c)* fees *d)* tax.

81

3 The man wheezed. He a) breathed with difficulty b) smoked c) moved quickly d) said very little.
4 There was a *stale* smell. It was a) strong b) not strong c) old d) fresh.
5 The bed *sagged*. It a) sank in the middle b) looked dirty c) gave off a smell d) seemed too small.
6 The wallpaper was *stained*. It a) had no colour b) was very old c) had dark, dirty marks d) was torn.

Use of English 1
In this conversation, Mr Hill's sentences are not complete. Finish them. He is talking to Jean at the agency before she goes to the room described in the passage.

Mr Hill: Now, what sort of room ___?
Jean: Something with a shower in it and cooking facilities, too.
Mr Hill: I see. And how much ___?
Jean: Not very much, I'm afraid. I'm only a student.
Mr Hill: Well, could you ___?
Jean: Certainly no more than £15 a week!
Mr Hill: And what sort of area ___?
Jean: Anywhere near the centre, if possible.
Mr Hill: Well, I'm afraid it will be very hard to find you anything but I'll see ___.

Use of English 2
Finish each sentence so that it means the same as the one above it.

Jean wanted a room near the centre of town because she went to an Art College there.
The reason . . .

Several minutes went by before the man came to the door.
It took . . .

It was difficult for him to get up the stairs.
The man had . . .

The room needed a clean more than anything else.
What . . .

It was the most depressing room Jean had ever seen.
Jean had . . .

In fact, the whole house depressed her.
In fact, she found . . .

She had to share the lavatory with others, which she disliked.
She disliked . . .

Mr Cartwright had had the room last.
The last person . . .

Showing that you are disappointed, that you expected something different

I'd expected the room to have a shower
I somehow thought there would be a shower
I'd been led to believe that there would be a shower

These are just a few of the ways of suggesting you thought things would be different. Use one of them to show you had expected a) a bigger room b) a separate lavatory c) better decoration d) more comfortable furniture e) more light in the room.

Now suppose you have just arrived at a 'holiday hotel' far from the beach, overcrowded and terrible rooms. What are some of the things you might say?

3.9 Interprop Limited

Questions

What do you think is happening here?

What kind of work do you think is done in this office?

Give reasons why you think it unlikely that this is *a*) a bank   *b*) a doctor's office   *c*) the headquarters of a large international company.

Suppose you had to work in this office; would you be happy or unhappy? Why?

What improvements would you suggest?

Talking points

Which do you think is better: working for someone else or being 'your own boss'? Why?

If you have a job now, describe a typical working day from the time you get up to the time you come home again.

You have a chance to learn English either by   *a*) studying in a language school in England or   *b*) getting a job in an office there and working. Which do you think the better way? Give reasons.

Listening comprehension and related practice

You are going to hear a passage about a girl called Alice, who applies for a job in an office. Listen to the passage twice. Then do the exercises.

1 The job seemed right for Alice because   *a*) she had lived in France and Spain   *b*) it involved a lot of travel to those places   *c*) she had a knowledge of several languages   *d*) she liked French and Spanish people.
2 When she got to the office, she found   *a*) she had come earlier than expected   *b*) she was on time but Jepley was late   *c*) Jepley had had to go out for half an hour   *d*) nobody expected her at all.
3 From the passage we learn that   *a*) the job would only be temporary   *b*) Alice had been in a car smash-up   *c*) Jepley had been in a car smash-up   *d*) Alice already had a job.
4 The passage suggests that Jepley was   *a*) not very busy nor really interested   *b*) far too busy to do the interview well   *c*) young and very overworked   *d*) busy most of the time but not then.
5 What sort of business was the company in?   *a*) we are not told   *b*) buying and selling land and houses   *c*) international banking   *d*) temporary jobs for secretaries.
6 At the end Alice decided to   *a*) wait and think about the offer   *b*) turn the job down   *c*) accept it only on a temporary basis   *d*) accept it.

Vocabulary

Listen to the passage once more. Tell the teacher to stop each time you think you have heard a word or phrase that means the same as the explanations below.

a) a kind of letter, very short   b) on time   c) opening the mouth sleepily   d) come in casually, as if nothing mattered   e) do someone else's work on a temporary basis   f) great surprise   g) slightly surprised   h) get (information) with great difficulty   i) buying and selling of land, houses, etc.   j) slightly angrily.

Getting people to be more precise

I wonder if you could tell me exactly ...
Could you be more specific about ...
I think I'd like to know a bit more about ...

You are trying to prise information out of Mr Jepley. His answers are always vague and unclear. Turn the questions below into ones that insist on precise information.

How much is the salary?
What kind of work am I supposed to do?
When do I have to be here every morning?
What kind of business does this company do?
How long are the holidays?
What sort of people do you work with?
What does the term 'personal assistant' mean?

Use of English
Miss Carson is the manager of a large shop. Bill, a young man, has just applied for the job of van driver. Complete Miss Carson's questions.

Miss Carson: Have you ever ___?
Bill: Yes, I drove a van for a big firm in London last year.
Miss Carson: And how long ___?
Bill: Well, a few months. You know.
Miss Carson: I'm sorry, but could you ___?
Bill: Well, I worked for them for six weeks, actually.
Miss Carson: I see. And why ___?
Bill: Well, they didn't like the way I drove the van and asked me to leave.
Miss Carson: But what exactly was wrong with ___?
Bill: They said I was careless.
Miss Carson: Careless? What exactly ___?
Bill: I had a few accidents.
Miss Carson: Hmm. I see. I'm sorry but I don't think ___.

Interaction
Study this advertisement carefully

> **FOREIGN STUDENTS IN ENGLAND**
>
> **Now is your chance to earn a lot of money**
>
> We are a large American publisher looking for sales people to sell our new self-study English courses to students in England. If you are already a student and want to earn a lot of money very easily come and meet our manager Mr Quickdollar who will be at the Royal Continental Hotel in London all next week, Room 2001, where he will interview.

You are a foreign student in England. You are talking to Mr Quickdollar. Exactly what questions would you ask him before you decided whether or not to take the job?

Composition
First discuss, then write out your idea of 'a good job'. Be sure to cover a) whether the job involves meeting a lot of people or not   b) indoors or outdoors, why?   c) holidays, salary (be realistic!)   d) for a big or a small firm? why? advantages and disadvantages of both.

3·10 ARRIVAL

Questions

Describe some of the things you think people are doing and saying here.

Do you think this is a very expensive or a rather cheap restaurant? Give reasons!

Describe all the things you have to do from the time you enter such a place to the time you leave it.

Talking points

A young businessman has to entertain some important customers. What are both the advantages and disadvantages for himself and *also for his wife* of *a)* eating in a restaurant like this   *b)* taking them to his home for a meal.

Try to describe some of the food you like very much.

Have you ever eaten any 'foreign' food? (English, American, etc.) What was your opinion of it? What did you like or dislike about it?

Listening comprehension and related practice

You are going to hear a passage about a couple called Tom and Carol. Listen at least twice. Then do the exercises.

1 When the story begins, Carol and Tom are   *a)* arguing about where to go that evening   *b)* trying to find a hotel in the country   *c)* looking for someone to give them directions   *d)* arguing about where they are.
2 It seems that just before the passage begins   *a)* they had a good meal in a big hotel   *b)* they came through a town with some hotels   *c)* they were told they could not stay at one hotel in a large town   *d)* they met a friend from London.
3 The hotel they want to stay at was a place   *a)* Tom had been to once before   *b)* both Tom and Carol had stayed at before   *c)* some of Tom's friends had recommended   *d)* Carol knew and disliked very much.
4 What do we learn about the weather?   *a)* It was dark but not too cold.   *b)* It was very dark and very cold.   *c)* Nothing at all.   *d)* It was damp and raining.
5 The man Tom spoke to did not at first give him directions because   *a)* Tom got the name of the hotel wrong   *b)* he was a stranger there himself   *c)* he was afraid of Tom   *d)* he was rather stupid.
6 When they finally arrived they found that   *a)* there was no room for them there   *b)* their room was not ready yet   *c)* they could eat but not stay there   *d)* everything was all right.

Interaction

Listen to the passage once more. Then imagine you are a friend of Carol's and that you are asking her about that evening. It is a few days after the

Listening
Comprehension
Passages

- This section contains the passages for Section Three.
- All these passages are recorded.
- The teacher will probably not play or read them to you in the order in which they occur here.

1 Escape from Hanley Park

And now for the rest of the news. Hanley Park Prison was the scene of a daring escape today. Here to tell us about it is Jeremy Allsop, our Birmigham Radio News reporter.

'At exactly 12.30 this afternoon a furniture lorry parked outside the prison wall. It is 18-feet high and in the sidestreet that runs outside the part of the prison where the main exercise yard is located. Over a hundred prisoners were there at the time.

Apparently two men climbed from the lorry through a hole in its roof and up a metal ladder to the top of the wall. They then immediately lowered two other ladders down to a small group of prisoners on the other side. As is now clear, this group of prisoners must have been informed of the exact details of the escape plan beforehand. Prison guards were at first prevented from reaching them by another group of prisoners, who began to riot. Several guards fought their way through them, and stopped all but two prisoners from climbing up the ladders. Of the two who managed to do so, one man fell after he had reached the top, hurting himself badly. The other, however, escaped in the lorry. Although a full-scale police alert was called only minutes after the escape, the lorry appears to have got away successfully. The prisoner who fell was left behind. Although police have not confirmed any details, it is understood he is now in hospital with a broken back. Order has been fully restored in the prison itself.'

2 A double life

For the last five years Colin Harrison has been leading a life which was described in court yesterday as 'a hellish nightmare of his own making'. Harrison, who is 34, met his first wife, Eileen, eight years ago. They soon had two children and Harrison seemed to settle down in a Bristol suburb to a 'solid, respectable life as a devoted husband and father'. His only apparent problem was his job as a long-distance lorry driver. This took him away for almost half of every month on long drives up to the northeast of England, particularly around the Newcastle area.

However, as the court learned, after three years of marriage, Harrison met another woman and fell in love with her. She was a pretty young widow, Mrs Claudia Paisley, whose husband had died in a tragic motor car accident two years earlier. Harrison married her as well, and began to lead a double life.

The first was in his home in Bristol, and the second was in the village of Ormley, near Newcastle, with his second wife. Neither of the two women knew of each other's existence. Harrison had two more children in his first marriage, the last of which, a boy, was born nine months ago. His second wife, Claudia, bore him a daughter around the same time. She already had two children from her earlier marriage.

In order to support his two families, Harrison had to work almost every hour of the day and night. In addition to his main job he took on a number of part-time jobs in both Bristol and Ormley. It became so bad that several months ago he suffered a complete physical and mental collapse. One of his doctors, to whom Harrison confessed everything, advised him to give himself up and then try to make a completely fresh start in life. Harrison took the advice. Yesterday, after pleading guilty to bigamy, he was given a two-year jail sentence, suspended for four years. The court heard that his first wife is now seeking a divorce.

3 Prince Albert and the jewel robbers

After living and working in London for more than a year, Linda still felt terribly lonely. She had done all sorts of things in order to make friends, but still had none. She had even joined the sports club of the large insurance company where she worked as a secretary, and had taken lessons in things like Badminton and even Judo. But despite all that her only real friend was Prince Albert, or Prince for short. And he was a rather foolish-looking mongrel dog. He belonged to the old woman who rented Linda a room in her huge, old-fashioned house.

Linda often took Prince out for a walk on Saturday mornings, which was when she did her week-end shopping. One day they were in a small side-street just round the corner from all the shops when Prince suddenly pulled Linda towards a lamp post. There was a large four-door car parked there. Linda noticed the man at the wheel. He looked nervous, almost frightened. Prince started sniffing round the lamp post. The man stared at him and then at Linda as if they had no right to be there. 'Hey! You! Clear off! Don't come near this car! Understand!' he said in a low but clear and threatening voice. Then he added a few highly insulting, four-letter words. Linda looked at him angrily and was just about to say something when she heard another voice behind her. 'Get away from that car!' It was a man who had just come running round a corner. Prince began to bark at this second stranger. He was on a lead and pulled Linda past the lamp post. The second man was carrying a large bag which he swung furiously at Prince. Prince leapt at him. Somehow the lead got entangled round the man's feet and he fell, hitting his head on the lamp post with a sickening thud and knocking himself unconscious.

Linda gaped. Then she felt herself being pushed from behind. It was the man in the car who had jumped out and was trying to shove her out of the way so that he could get the bag the man was carrying. But Linda thought she was being attacked and, suddenly remembering her judo, threw him over her shoulder. He hit the pavement hard and sprawled there, winded. Just then a police car came racing round the corner. Two policemen jumped out. They gaped, too. Then they fell upon both men and handcuffed them. One of the policemen looked at Linda in amazement and said, 'I don't know whether you know it but you've just stopped a big jewel robbery. One of these men robbed a jeweller's shop a minute ago. The other one must have been waiting to drive him away in that car!'

4 The Prize (1)

I grew up in a small town in the West of England. I cannot tell you very much about my father. He was a journalist and was hardly ever at home and then, when I was eleven, went away to fight in the First World War. But he must have been a pleasant man, with an enormous sense of humour, and my mother must have loved him enormously. I can remember hearing them laughing a lot when I was in bed. I remember the years of the war very well. I had just started going to grammar school when it began. All the teachers were very old. The young ones were in the Army. We were often hungry, particularly towards the end of the war, but our old teachers never seemed to notice. We had to translate meaningless verses from the Latin and Greek classics. I remember doing translations from Homer. The teachers seemed closer to the Trojan War than to the one going on in France a few hundred miles away. It seemed stupid to me, even then. My father was killed in Belgium, at Passchendale, in 1918. Passchendale, as you perhaps know, was one of the worst and bloodiest battles of the whole horrible war. A lot of soldiers on both sides drowned in the mud and rain, or died of illness. But we still had to translate Greek and Latin at school. I have hated those languages and the idea of war ever since. My mother died in 1919, a year after the war ended. She died in the great influenza epidemic that killed so many people all over Europ in that year. I was raised by a religious aunt. She went to church every morning, always talked about how God loved us all. She never seemed to show me any love herself, and I never showed her any.

5 The Prize (2)   By the time the Second World War began, I had already travelled abroad a great deal. I had studied for two years at a German university and later had worked as a journalist in the Far East, particularly in Japan. I had made a great many friends in those places. Suddenly, many of them became 'the enemy'. It was as if a black curtain had been drawn between them and me.

One night in 1941, around Christmas time, I was with an anti-aircraft crew near the mouth of the Thames. I was writing a newspaper article about our air defences. Further up the river a town was being bombed. We could see the flames. Even the bombs could be heard. They sounded like huge kettle drums that were being tuned for a concert. Then we were warned that some of the bombers were coming our way. Shortly afterwards we heard their engines. Two powerful searchlights criss-crossed on one of them just above us. Our guns began firing. They were so loud in my ears that I felt as though I were actually inside one of those drums. Suddenly I saw a flicker of flame inside the aircraft. It looked almost as if someone had lit a match up there. The flame suddenly spread. The anti-aircraft crew began to cheer. I almost did so myself. It was rather like watching a film. Nothing seemed real. The bomber looked like a fly in a spider's net.

But then I realised that the men up in that bomber were human beings. They had flesh that could burn, voices that could scream and bodies that could be smashed and broken. I suddenly wondered if some of them were the brothers or sons of friends of mine, or even my friends themselves. It is not easy to hate people whose names you know, whose language you speak and with whom you have laughed and drunk. They had been dropping bombs on us a moment ago. But they could hardly have known just what they were doing. Later, other friends of mine in different bombers would die in the same way over Germany and Japan. They would kill innocent people just as the men up in that blazing bomber had done. It was as though we were all puppets in a mad play. So much was wasted. So much life was lost that could never be replaced. And so I did not and could not cheer as I watched that bomber crash. There were no parachutes. All the bomber crew must have died.

6 The Prize (3)   I live in fear of boredom. That is, I live in fear of boring others. Formal speeches can so easily bore, particularly if they are long. Mine will be very short and I hope simple.

In my novels I have always tried to use simple language to describe some of the reality I have seen. For many years I was a journalist and I happened to see at first hand many of the terrible events that have dominated our century. And in the novels I tried to convey something of the experience simple people had of those events. I keep saying 'simple'. There is of course nothing simple about being an innocent civilian terrified out of your wits as bombers fly above you trying to kill you and destroy your home. There is nothing simple about being a soldier equally terrified that you will be killed in a battle. It is not simple to go years without work or proper food. It is not simple to starve.

But I have still tried to use simple words because I know how much easier it is to lie with more complicated ones. As George Orwell pointed out, if I say something like 'My government has determined on the undertaking of a low-risk operation in order to pacify several areas of disorder in a remote part of an undeveloped and hostile country' it sounds much better than saying 'We are going to kill off some villagers and other peasants. They probably can't defend themselves anyway. This will teach them not to cause us any trouble!'

Using simple language is not the same as making things more simple than they really are. Reality is never simple. But it is better to try to describe it fully and simply. Perhaps that way we can get at the truth. But we should never be satisfied that we 'know the truth'. Another writer – a German – his name was Lessing – pointed out that it was not the possession of the truth that made us truly human. We might become arrogant, proud and lazy if we thought we really knew the truth. What makes us human, then, is not the truth but the sincere and honest search for it, and the knowledge that we can never really know the complete and whole truth about anything. Only fanatics think they can do that. All I have tried to do in my books is to get at the truth behind some of the things I have seen, and to describe it as fully and as simply as I can. And always I have known that truth itself is a terribly complex and many-sided thing. And now I wish only to express my deep gratitude for the great honour you have shown me in the form of this prize. Those are simple but I assure you deeply-felt words. Thank you.

7 A slight emergency

We had hardly got above the clouds over the airport when a calm voice said over the loudspeaker:

'For technical reasons we shall be returning immediately to London Airport. Please keep your seatbelts fastened.'

I was rather surprised and glanced at the old lady next to me. She had been very chatty while we were waiting to take off.

'I'm going to New York to visit some relatives there. I always sleep wonderfully well whenever I get into a plane,' she had told me.

And indeed, she seemed to be in a very deep sleep already.

Just then a passenger behind me shouted.

'Oh, my God! The wing's on fire.'

I looked out of the window and my blood froze. Smoke and flames were pouring out of one of the engines. The plane was already turning and losing altitude fast.

'What's happening? Are we going to crash?' an American in front of me demanded. The cabin crew were already moving up and down the aisle, reassuring people, saying things like:

'It's all right. There's no need to worry. Now, if you just sit still, everything will be all right. Don't get up. Don't get upset.'

I looked out again. The ground was rushing up at us with sickening speed. We were already so low that I could make out cars and even people.

'It's only a slight emergency,' a stewardess told me with a strained smile.

Suddenly there was a sickening bump and we were rushing along the runway at a terrifying speed. The brakes screeched. The engines roared even more loudly. We came to a shuddering stop. The cabin crew flung open emergency exits and the passengers began sliding down huge, stocking-like chutes to the ground. A fire engine was already putting out the fire in that one engine. I had to shake the old lady violently to wake her up.

'What's wrong? Surely the journey isn't over already! I mean, have we got to New York?' she asked sleepily.

8 The room

Jean knocked and waited. After a while a short, middle-aged man, unshaven and in carpet slippers, opened the door.

'The agency sent me. They told me you had a vacant room,' Jean explained. He stared at her suspiciously for a moment, looking at her up and down.

'It's . . . at the top of the stairs . . . three flights up,' he finally said. He turned. Joan understood she was to follow him. He coughed and wheezed as they climbed past door after door, all with numbers on them.

'Of course, the room needs a bit of a clean. Hasn't been lived in for a time. Understand?'

Jean nodded. They were standing in front of a door marked '13'. He pushed it and she walked through. The room was small and dark. There was the same smell of stale cabbage and cooking oil she had noticed in the hallway. The old wooden bed sagged under a dusty-looking mattress and a pile of greyish blankets. The wallpaper was the colour of oatmeal and was stained and seemed to be coming off the wall in places. The carpet had once been red but never very thick.

'I . . . I was told there was a shower or something like that,' Jean said. The man simply pointed to an old, cracked washbasin with a dripping tap in the corner.

'And . . . and the lavatory?'

'Down the hall. Share it with the others on this floor.'

For a moment Jean couldn't think of anything to say. The man broke in.

'Old Mr Cartwright really liked this room.'

'Mr Cartwright? Who . . . who's he?'

'The old man who had this room last. He died right there, on that bed.'

9 Interprop Limited

Alice had seen the advertisement and applied for the job. It seemed ideal for her. She knew French and Spanish very well and was learning German. A few days later she got a note from a Mr Jepley at Interprop asking her to appear for an interview on Wednesday at 2.30 promptly. 'He's out but he'll be back in a little while,' the receptionist said with a yawn when Alice got there. Half an hour went by. Then at three o'clock Jepley breezed in after an obviously alcoholic lunch. He disappeared for a few more minutes and then motioned her in.

'Already got a job, I see,' he said, glancing at her application.

'Yes, but it's only temporary. The regular girl's in hospital after a car smash-up, and I'm filling in for her,' Alice explained.

Jepley seemed young to be the director of such a company, which was what the title on his door said he was. And the offices themselves, although well-furnished, seemed rather small for an 'international company'.

'All right. You'll do,' Jepley suddenly said.

Alice stared at him in astonishment. She had expected the interview to be less casual.

'What? You mean you're offering me the job?' she asked.

'That's right. If you want it.' Jepley yawned just as the receptionist had done. He rubbed his eyes, which had bags under them. Alice was pretty sure he had not got them from overworking.

'Well, I think I'd like to find out a bit more about the job first!' she said emphatically. Jepley looked puzzled. Gradually she prised some information out of him. It turned out that the company specialised in international property deals. The salary was good; much better in fact than the one she was getting in her temporary job.

'Well? What about it?' Jepley asked, rather irritably.

Alice could not make up her mind at first and was very hesitant. But finally, after deciding she had nothing to lose, she nodded.

10 Arrival

'Are you sure you're even on the right road?' Carol asked. She could feel a headache coming on – the sort she got when she went too long without eating. Tom grunted and said nothing.

'I don't see why we couldn't have stayed in one of the hotels in that town we came through a few moments ago. It would have been much simpler if we had. I mean, we'd probably be sitting down to a good meal by now!'

Tom still said nothing. They were driving along a narrow country road. The cold, damp winter evening had already closed in, and the heater in the car wasn't working properly. Carol's hands and feet felt as if they were made of ice.

'After all, you don't even seem to know the name of this place your friends in London say is so wonderful!'

Just then they came to a village. Tom stopped the car when he saw a man walking down the street. He rolled down the window. The bitterly cold air came rushing in. His breath rose in puffs of steam as he spoke.

'Excuse me, but is there a hotel named "The Dark Owl" somewhere around here?'

'The Dark Owl?'

The man had a blank look on his face and looked very doubtful.

'Yes, "The Dark . . . something-or-other". Some kind of bird.'

Suddenly the man's face lit up.

'Oh, you mean "The Black Eagle"! Look! Do you see that bridge? Just follow the road over it. You go through a kind of forest and then up a hill. You'll see it just in front of you!'

They drove on for a few minutes. Suddenly they saw a large house in front of them. It looked like an old manor. There were lights on in most of the rooms. They stopped in front of it and through one of the large windows Carol could see a huge room with a roaring fire in it. People were already sitting down to dinner. White-coated waiters moved among them with steaming, silver dishes. She could smell the sweet odour of the wood fire. Tom got out, went into Reception and came back in a few seconds.

'It's all right. Our room's ready. It's very warm inside. Come on.'

experience. Find out about *a)* the weather that evening *b)* how she felt *c)* how they finally found the hotel (who did they ask, where, etc.) *d)* exactly where the hotel was *e)* what the hotel itself was like.

Vocabulary
Find the *one* best answer.

1. Tom *grunted*. He *a)* got angry *b)* agreed *c)* made a motion with his head *d)* made a kind of noise.
2. A meal is *a)* a kind of drink *b)* breakfast, lunch or dinner *c)* a place to sit *d)* a place to rest.
3. There was a *blank look* on the man's face. In other words, he *a)* looked stupid *b)* looked foolish *c)* clearly did not understand *d)* was angry.
4. A *manor* is a *a)* special kind of hotel *b)* place for men only *c)* place for men and women to stay together *d)* kind of large house that had probably once belonged to a lord.
5. An *odour* is *a)* any kind of smell *b)* a very sweet smell *c)* a very bad smell *d)* a very difficult thing to smell.

Suggesting that someone has made a mistake

I can't understand why you . . .
It would've been better if you hadn't . . .
I don't think you should have . . .

You are Carol. Use one of these forms to suggest to Tom that he was wrong to *a)* drive through the town without stopping *b)* take the last turning *c)* reserve a room at the hotel at all *d)* listen to his friends' advice *e)* come so far *f)* go to the hotel.

Open-ended dialogue
This scene might have occurred between Tom and the clerk in reception. What do you think Tom is saying?

Tom: ___
Clerk: No, sir. I'm afraid there's no room reserved for anybody of that name.
Tom: ___
Clerk: You did? By phone? Well, exactly who did you speak to?
Tom: ___
Clerk: Because if you could remember, sir, I might be able to speak to the person who took your reservation and find out why there's no room for you now.
Tom: ___
Clerk: Yes, sir, I realise you're upset but I assure you, there's no room reserved for you. Here. Look at the list yourself.
Tom: ___
Clerk: Yes, as it happens there are several large hotels near here. They're all in Clapbridge. That's the town you probably passed through on your way here.
Tom: ___
Clerk: Well, I'm sorry you feel that way, sir. I apologise but there's nothing we can do.

Use of English
Rewrite each sentence without changing the basic meaning. Begin as shown.

Carol wished they had stopped in Clapbridge.
Carol would have preferred . . .

She had gone a long time without eating.
It had been a long time . . .

She was angry with Tom because he had not stopped.
She was angry with Tom for . . .

She was sure she would freeze to death if they did not stop soon.
Unless . . .

With the help of a stranger, they found the hotel.
A stranger helped . . .

ACKNOWLEDGEMENTS

We are grateful to Ivan Lapper for the illustrations on pages 1, 3, 7, 11, 15, 19, 23, 27, 31, 35, 39, 43, 67, 69, 71, 73, 75 and 77.

We are grateful to the following for permission to reproduce copyright photographs:

Barnaby's Picture Library for pages 79, 81; Camera Press Ltd., for pages 43, 83.

Cover photographs by Camera Press Ltd., (top); Trust Houses Forte Ltd., (bottom).